DISCOURSES ON

AITAREYA UPANIṢAD

Original Upaniṣad Text in Devanāgarī
with Transliteration in Roman letters,
Word - for - Word meaning in Text order

with

Translation

and

Commentary

by

Swami Chinmayananda

CENTRAL CHINMAYA MISSION TRUST
MUMBAI

Published	number of times upto 1983				
Edition		1982	-	5000	copies
Edition		1992	-	3000	copies
Revised Edition		1998	-	1000	copies
Reprint	September	2000	-	1000	copies
Reprint	September	2001	-	2000	copies
Reprint	December	2004	-	2000	copies
Reprint	October	2007	-	1000	copies

Published by:
Central Chinmaya Mission Trust
Sandeepany Sadhanalaya
Saki Vihar Road, Mumbai - 400 072. India.
Tel.: 091-22-2857 2367, 2857 5806
Fax: 091-22-2857 3065
Email : ccmt@vsnl.com
Website : www.chinmayamission.com

Distribution Centre in USA:
Chinmaya Mission West
Publications Division
560 Bridgetown Pike,
Langhorne, PA 19053, USA
Tel.: (215)396-0390 Fax: (215)396-9710
www.chinmayapublications.org
publications@chinmaya.org

Printed by:
Sagar Unlimited
Unit No. 1, Y.A.C. Industrial Estate,
Kondivita Lane,
Andheri (E), Mumbai - 400 059
Tel.: 022-28362777 / 30829777
Email: somik@vsnl.net

Price: Rs. 50/-

ISBN: 81-7597-055-3

Contents

Preface to the Revised Edition

We all know that much of our ancient literature is now extinct. There were as many as 1180 *Śākhā-s* of *Vedik* literature. It is believed that each School had one *Upaniṣad* attached to it. Of about 280 *Upaniṣad-s* unearthed so far, 108 have been generally accepted as authentic texts. Out of these, eleven viz., *Īśa, Kena, Kaṭha, Praśna, Muṇḍaka, Māṇḍūkya, Taitirīya, Aitareya, Chāndogya, Bṛhadāraṇyaka and Śvetāśvatara,* in that order, have been commented upon by the recent master-minds *Ācāryā-s* like *Śrī Śaṅkara, Rāmānuja* and *Madhavācārya,* and are thus classified as 'Major' or Principal *Upaniṣad-s.* Some do not accept commentary on the *Śvetāśvatara Upaniṣad* as that of *Śaṅkara Bhagavatpāda and* thus acknowledge only ten as 'Major' *Upaniṣad-s.*

The other *Upaniṣad-s* are considered as 'Minor'—not on account of their contents, or in the depth of their thoughts, or in the completeness of their exposition but because no commentaries are available from the great *Ācāryā*-s. The new initiates are generally prescribed these minor *Upaniṣad-s* only after a thorough study of the exhaustive commentaries *(Bhāṣyā-s)* by the great Masters on five or six of the Major *Upaniṣad-s.* Thus, these became 'minor' only with reference to the knowledge the students have already acquired as a result of their study of the "main" *Upaniṣad-s* and their reflection on these 'minor' ones serves as an interesting revision of the knowledge already gathered.

All *Upaniṣad-s*—Major or Minor enunciate the one goal which is liberation and prescribe techniques of achieving that goal—are of equal importance and value. The classification major or minor—is only to distinguish the well-known ones commented upon by *Śaṅkarācārya.*

The super-human genius, that was *Veda Vyāsa,* for the first time, gathered *Vedik mantrā-s,* recorded in written language, and classified the entire wealth of *Vedik* knowledge into four volumes in a harmonious rythm, both in the arrangement and classification of contents. Each *Veda* was further divided into broad three sections—*Mantrā-s, Brāhmaṇā-s* and *Āraṇyakā-s.*

The *mantra* portion contains expressions of wonderment, joy and ecstasy at the choking visions of beauty in nature's exuberance. They worshipped through the *mantrā-s* the dignity of the mountain, the majesty of the sun-rise, the beauty of the moon, the grandeur of the occean and such other phenomenal powers.

The second section i.e., *Brāhmaṇa* portion contains detailed and scientific description of methods of various ritualistic performances and secret methods to invoke the Mighty Powers behind the nature to bless the devotees' desires into fulfilment. This section is further divided into two sub-sections—*Karma Kāṇḍa* and *Upāsanā Kāṇḍa.* The grosser rituals, their rules, prescriptions for various *Yajñā-s* and *Yāgā-s* form the first sub-section, while comparatively subtler meditations, that are part and parcel of *Vedik* ritualism, form the second sub-section.

The last section is called *Āraṇakā-s* (*Araṇya* means forest)—that can be studied only in the quiet *Himālayan* Valleys in a mental climate of psychological and intellectual retirement from the stormy passions and desires. This section is also known as *Upaniṣad-s* or *Vedānta* (*Veda* + *anta* i.e., the end of *Vedā-s*) as the literal meaning connotes comprises of the philosophical portion of the *Vedā-s.*

The *Aitareyopaniṣad,* also called *Bahvṛcopaniṣad,* belongs to *Ṛg Veda* and forms the 4th, 5th and 6th chapters of the second *Āraṇyaka* of *Aitareya Brāhmaṇa*. The 5th and 6th chapter i.e., *Ānanda Vallī* and *Bhṛgu Vallī* put together are also known as *Vāruṇī Upaniṣad*. While earlier portion of the *Brāhmaṇa* deals with the *Karma* as associated with meditation, the *Aitareya Upaniṣad* is concerned only with the knowledge of the Self.

Śaṅkara calls it *"Ātma Ṣaṭka."* Prima facie, there are only five sections in this *Upaniṣad, Śaṅkara* considers the concluding *Śānti Mantra* as an independent section to make it *Ṣaṭka* (i.e., six). The four *Vedā-s* have one Major text or *Mahā Vākya* each. The importance of *Aitareya Upaniṣad* can very well be gauged from the fact that the *Mahā Vākya of Ṛg Veda—Prajñānam Brahma i.e., "Consciousness is Brahman"* is found in this *Upaniṣad* (III-i-3).

It is one of the few *Upaniṣad-s* where author—the *Guru-Ṛṣi* is known—*Mahidāsa Aitareya.* His father was a *brāhmaṇa* named *Viśāla* and mother was *Itarā* (lit. meaning the other). The story of how *Mahidāsa* was denied the privilege of sitting in the lap of his father is narrated in the Introduction. *Itarā,* who was perhaps from the potter community noticed the sad plight of her son and prayed to her *Iṣṭa Devatā* i.e., Goddess Earth, who appeared in a Divine form, placed *Mahidāsa* in a celestial seat and imparted unrivalled Wisdom. Thus was born, out of the potter *Mahidāsa,* the Proletarian *Ṛṣi,* the Sage of the Labourers, and Son of the Soil Seer *Aitareya,* who attained God-hood and authored this scripture of the common-man and sang the song of *Hindū* culture from a hut of the 'slum.'

In his commentary on *Śānti Pāṭha, Gurudeva* enunciates a simple technique of enhancing memory and asserts that the capacity for remembering all previous discourses is acquired through a self-conscious and deliberate effort. Memory is facilitated by continuously employing the mind to dwell upon those thoughts for a long period, and this mental and intellectual process of assimilation of what we have heard is called "Reflection" (*manan*).

The *Upaniṣad* begins with the assertion that "in the beginning *Ātmā (*Self) alone was this Universe." Here *Ātmā* (Self) is nothing other than the All-pervading Reality ... *Brahman*—for there is no difference between the cup-space and the universal outer-space, argues the Master.

Creation is but a super-imposition upon the Truth, just as the appearance of the *ghost* on the *post.* The Creation is beginning-less is explained in a most simple and easily understandable flawless logic by *Pūjya Gurudeva.*

"Even the Creator is not free to create a world as He likes," is a startling assertion which is explained in a masterly analogy. Just as a contractor would construct a house to his client's blue-print, the Creator is bound by the total *Vāsanā-s* in the cosmos in creating the world, wherein all the *vāsanā-s* can find a field to express themselves. We with our actions—known and unknown, conscious and unconscious—are making the blue-prints of our future. The Lord is but a contractor who executes our plans, as we give it to Him, asserts the Master.

After creating worlds, its guardians—the presiding deities were created. The deities i.e., the gods desired abode and food. The body could not remain without the Creator, so the Creator entered from *Nāndana*—the highest gate—the suture of the skull. Having entered, the Conscious Principle revels in us in three states of experiences i.e., waking, dream and deep-sleep-state. That which makes things available for our perception and understanding is 'Consciousness.' He is called *Idamdara*; since gods are fond of their cryptic names—he is indirectly called as *Indra*, says the *Ṛṣi.*

The two pronouns "that" and "this" are very simply explained for even a layman to grasp. The point which is near to us is indicated by "this," while the one which is farther from us is known by "that." That Subjective Centre—which is nearest to us, so near that there is no other point with reference to which, It can never be "that"—is best defined as "this," explains the Master.

The *Upaniṣad* provides a definite internal proof, if one is needed, that the *Hindū* women, in the hoary past, had free access to the great teachers to learn *Vedā-s*. The importance of pre-natal education, which is of most recent origin in the west, was highly developed, valued and enforced by the ancient sages. They laid great emphasis not only entertaining purely *sāttvik* thoughts during pregnancy, but also eliminating even a chance sensual thought in a pregnant woman.

This is reflected in the injunction "Pregnant women, please retire," while the teacher explains the three births of man—first, when he pours seed into the womb of his wife; second, when the woman nourishes her embryo within her and the father nourishes both i.e., his wife and the embryo within her; and the third, when the father having reached a ripe old age dies away and is born again.

The teacher is thus pointing at the chord of oneness on which are strung the past, the present and the future. The father representing the past, the son—the present, and the third birth of the father—the future generation. The birth and death are only with reference to the body, in its essence the spirit is the theme of the *Upaniṣad*, affirms the Master.

The *Hindū* mode of pre-natal education is provided through a *Paurāṇik* story: the *Asura* king *Hiraṇyakaśipu* through severe austerities had obtained a comprehensive boon from *Brahmā*, which made him almost invincible—"he could not be killed by striking or throwing weapons, by enemies, by thunderbolts or by dried tree-trunks or by high mountains or by water or fire; he could not be killed by Gods, *Daityā-s*, *Seers*, *siddhā-s*, nor by any other beings created by *Brahmā*; he could not be slain in the heaven or earth, in daytime or at night, in-doors or out-doors, from above or below." Not satisfied by such a consummate boon, he set out for further austerities which naturally disturbed the denizens of heaven.

To complete this side of the story first—lord *Viṣṇu* had to take a fuzzy *Nara-Siṁha* (Man-lion) *Avatāra* having a marvellous form with fierce and fiery eyes, matted locks and quivering manes, projecting tusks and sword-like sharp tongue equiped with claws and other unique weapons (neither man nor animal) and tore apart his body with a razor-sharp claws (without any weapon) after placing him on his knees (which is neither above or below), on the threshold (which is neither in nor out), at dusk (which was neither day nor night).

To continue the main story, gods being alarmed at *Hiraṇyakaśipu's* intention of acquiring further powers through *tapasyā,* thought of saving the society by preventing the next generation from being turned into felons (*Ātatāyin-s*) and planned to provide pre-natal education to all pregnant women in *Hiraṇyakaśipu's* kingdom, at that time.

The great consort of *Hiraṇyakaśipu* too was pregnant and *Nārada*—the Sage of Wisdom and Devotion conducted her to *Vasiṣṭha Āśrama* where she remained in the serene atmosphere, till the fullness of her pregnancy listening to daily discourses and serving the *Āśrama,* resulting in the birth of the boy of our *Purāṇā-s,* the devoted *Prahlāda.*

The *Ṛṣi* comes to the most important Major Text of the *Upaniṣad*—nay of the *Ṛg Veda* itself, when the teacher thunders that "Consciousness is *Brahman*" (*Prajñānam Brahma*), and concludes the *Upaniṣad* with a bang.

Repeated reprints had resulted in numerous inaccuracies rendering understanding difficult for new *Sādhakā-s.* Besides readability was poor in small print. Both these aspects are taken care of in the revised layout, the credit for which is due to Shri Vishwamitra Puri who with consistent perseverance and devotion scrutinised the entire book very minutely to identify misprints, missing words and lines; added diacritical marks and pursued steadfastly, the suggested changes/improvements, with the *Ācārya* of *Sāndīpany* Mumbai for approval.

In this revised Edition diacritical marks are used for Transliteration of *Saṁskṛta* words in the verses as well as commentary. In the 'word-for-word meaning' section also, for benefit of readers not knowing *Devanāgarī,* transliteration of *Saṁskṛta* words is added. Non-English words have been italicised. In the 'free translation' section where the entire text is italicised, to distinguish *Saṁskṛta* words, 'normal' fonts are used. This will help readers to identify and pronounce the words correctly.

The English plural sign 's' has been added to the untranslated *Saṁskṛta* words after a hyphen (-) to show that it is not elemental to the word e.g., *mantrā-s, Vedā-s, Ṛṣī-s* etc. Macrons are used on the last letter e.g. *'ā, ī'* of such words to lengthen the quantity of sound in consonance with the pronunciation.

To be true to the *Saṁskṛta* text in transliteration, we have used "*brāhmaṇa*" for the first *Varṇa* instead of the commonly used word "*brāhmin.*" It need not be confused with the term "*Brahman*" of the *Vedāntin*-s.

A key to the transliteration and pronunciation is added in the beginning and Alphabetical Index to *Mantrā*-s at the end of the book. Some of the verses are split in the commentary. To fecilitate easy location of split portions as well as other important lines, quotable statements occuring in the *Upaniṣad,* a Supplementary Alphabetical Index is provided at the end.

We are pleased to bring out the present revised Edition of the original commentary given by *H. H. Svāmī Chinmayānanda* whom we all reverentially refer as *Pūjya Gurudeva.* This is our humble offering at His holy feet with a prayer that may His words and guidance inspire us to carry on His work in all spheres of activities such as this---publication of scriptural thoughts for the benefit of society.

Śrī Buddha Pūrṇimā, the 11th May, 1998 **Publishers**

Preface to the Second Edition

In this Edition, diacritical marks are used for Transliteration of *Saṁskṛta* words in the *Mantra*'s and commentary. Non-English words have been Italicised. This will help readers to identify and pronounce the words correctly. For easier reading, lines in *Mantra*'s are split and re-arranged.

Untranslated *Saṁskṛta* words are put within inverted commas and then English plural sign 's' is added to show that it is not elemental to the word e.g., '*Veda*'s, '*Mantra*'s etc.

A key to the Transliteration and Pronunciation has been added in the beginning of the book. A list of 'Contents' has also been added to the present Edition.

Date : 13th April, 1992. **Publishers**

TRANSLITERATION AND PRONUNCIATION GUIDE

ॐ	oṁ	home	ॐ	oṁ	Rome
अ	a	fun	ट	ṭa	touch
आ	ā	car	ठ	ṭha	ant-hill
इ	i	pin	ड	ḍa	duck
ई	ī	feet	ढ	ḍha	godhood
उ	u	put	ण	ṇa	thunder
ऊ	ū	pool	त	ta	(close to) think
ऋ	ṛ	rig	थ	tha	(close to) pathetic
ॠ	ṝ	(long ṛ)	द	da	(close to) father
ऌ	ḷ	*	ध	dha	(close to) breathe hard
ए	e	play	न	na	numb
ऐ	ai	high	प	pa	purse
ओ	o	over	फ	pha	sapphire
औ	au	cow	ब	ba	but
अं	aṁ	**	भ	bha	abhor
अः	aḥ	***	म	ma	mother
क	ka	kind	य	ya	young
ख	kha	blockhead	र	ra	run
ग	ga	gate	ल	la	luck
घ	gha	log-hut	व	va	virtue
ङ	ṅa	sing	श	śa	shove
च	ca	chunk	ष	ṣa	bushel
छ	cha	match	स	sa	sir
ज	ja	jug	ह	ha	house
झ	jha	hedgehog	ळ	(Note 1)	(close to) world
ञ	ña	bunch	क्ष	kṣa	worksheet
त्र	tra	three	ज्ञ	jña	*
ऽ	'	unpronounced अ (a)	ऽऽ	"	Unpronounced आ (ā)

Note 1: " ḷ " itself is sometimes used.
** Nasalisation of the preceding vowel.

* No English Equivalent.
*** Aspiration of preceding vowel.

Introduction

Through an ill-adjusted telescope or microscope, we know, any object will, of necessity, look blurred with its details lost in a general confusion of data. The more we rightly focus the instrument, the clearer will become our appreciation and true evaluation of the perceived object. Similarly, our perception of the world outside is vague and our estimation of life false, when we bring into it a mal-adjusted mind-intellect equipment.

In this sense, if we compare the function of the mind and intellect with an ordinary telescope, we can say that the inner in us has the mind for its 'object-glass,' and the intellect for its 'eye-piece.' When the adjustments in each of them are not correct, and when their relationship with each other is not properly maintained, the object viewed does not faithfully represent its true form. The more perfect be their adjustments, is the better the vision through them.

When an individual has lived his life in integration with his mind through one or the other, or even a combination of the four main paths in spiritual practices, *Bhakti, Karma, Jñāna*, or *Haṭha* Yoga, that individual starts gaining a deeper and clearer vision of his 'life as a whole.' He is no longer available for any vulgar enthusiasm to sweep him away from himself and make him a victim of some of the passing fancies of his generation. He independently evaluates life and with a tragic poignancy comes to feel the dire imperfections that poison everything. He perceives the descent of a dark veil of tragic finitude upon the world around him making it ugly and insufferably detestable.

This does not mean that he turns himself cynical or that he becomes a victim of either a mental dejection or any intellectual pessimism. It only means that in his ruthless judgement he sees life—all the happenings without and within him, the lot of the people outside his home and the destiny of himself in his own family—in their stark nakedness bereft of all sentimentalities or aversions, as a scientist observes the rising Sun through his telescope.

The intellectual vision of the scientist is not clouded by the sentimental emotions of a poet or the deep discoveries of a mystic and his penetrating perception. The scientist observes a phenomenon and carefully notes down his observations of data. Similarly, when through right living and correct practices of devotion (*upāsanā*), a seeker gets fully integrated within, he comes to see things as they are, stripped naked of his attachments, vanities, pre-conceived mental dreams and their associated ideas.

Such a full grown *man-man* becomes a fully qualified student for the pursuit of Truth through the Path of Knowledge which *Vedānta* prescribes. Such an individual comes to see a purposeless hollowness in the business called "Life" as it is available for him in the world. He comes to wonder and conclude that life is "but an empty dream." At the same time his acute intelligence instinctively tells him that it cannot be so and that there must be some great purpose behind it all, which perhaps he is not able to perceive.

This restlessness of the soul, glowing at first as a mere intellectual quest, soon burns him up in a conflagration and roasted in this deep and subtle fire within, he becomes all ablaze with doubts and questions and seeks a solution of this great riddle called life

Men of knowledge in the world's secular fields are, no doubt, diligent *scientists in life*, but it is only the *Ṛṣī*-s, prophets and Masters who are the *Scientists of life*. To the material scientist the world of *matter* upto the outermost margins of the Spirit is the field, while to the great seers the deeper world within, the very spiritual realm—Life itself—is their field of enquiry. When modern scientists like Einstein, at certain moments of their wanderings, cross their frontiers and come to step over the realm of the philosophy, they come to enjoy the status of a prophet of their age. If Darwin was a prophet of the 19th Century in the West, and student of Physics would admit that Einstein was the prophet of the present century.

A seeker, therefore, approaches a Master and pours out his question of life and seeks to understand the logic of the happenings in it. The answers given by sympathetic Masters of love in the *verāṇḍā* of their hermitages, on the banks of the *Ganges*, are all traditionally handed down to us, and they constitute the text-books of the *Hindū* Philosophy.

Devoid of its relationship with life, a scripture becomes a dead book of idealism and not a dynamic philosophy which can bring hope and joy, succour and solace, to the generation of faithful followers. There must be, therefore, an intimate relationship between a dynamic religion and life, just as there should be a definite relationship set up between a musician and his accompaniments for good music, between the plant and the blossom on it so that they may become the source of fruits. When there is any revolutionary change in the religious ideologies and the philosophical concepts of a generation, the entire pattern of life in the society changes.

And at certain periods of history, when convulsions of social and economic change overtake a community, the existing religion also must be mobile enough in its non-essentials to swing and change, yield and accommodate, relax and embrace the new demands that have been created in the society under the new impulses set forth by the revolution. That religion which is not versatile enough to respond properly to these inner throbbings of a society or a community, will perish under the weight and sway of the on-rushing progress.

The epitaphs written on the tombs of all dead religions have the same theme; and if we are to make an honest report upon the working of some of the existing religions of the world with reference to the new born one-world awareness and the growing democratic appreciation of the equality of men, we can safely forecast that they are destined to die away soon. History of religions clearly indicates this intimate wed-lock between religion and life, but somehow or other, in our haste and hurry, in our impatience and ignorance, we come to question whether there is after all any relationship between life and religion.

Unlike the Semitic religions, *Hindūism* is not a rigid text-book of commandments and orders, declarations and revelations, but our sacred lore is a text-book of scientific facts and it has the healthy instincts of growing tradition. If a tree were to be encased in re-inforced concrete it cannot grow; no doubt, it must have a bark of some rigidity, but it must be a living bark that will yield freely to the healthy impulses of growth that may come from within the core of the tree. *Hindūism* as a Science of Life recognised this sacred fact and has refused to bind in folios together, but kept them all in loose sheets so that new insertions and rejections are always possible..... except, of course, some of the eternal laws and truths which are fundamental to life.

This healthy sign of accommodation and adjustments is nowhere so perceptibly seen as in the long and unbroken history of the brilliant culture and the inimitable spiritual vision of the *Hindū-s*.

The early *Āryan-s* marching through Afghanistan and crossing the N.W. Frontier migrated into the Punjab and this majestic procession of the earliest colonisers swept down and reached the Gangetic plain, where they settled down to thrive and grow into a distinct culture group wherein duty was more sacred than right, and intelligence more appreciated than emotions. The history of the growth of their philosophy to-day reads as a monumental saga of the best that man as an individual or as a community had ever accomplished in the history of the world.

The entire science of the spirit preserved through memory was handed down from generation to generation and it is called the *Vedā-s*. These observations on Life and declarations of the experienced-Truth were handed down from generation of Masters to a generation of their disciples, who, in their turn, handed them down to their disciples... and in this process as a river that gathers more and more water from its tributaries as it winds along its path to the sea, the *Hindū* tradition grew in bulk and details.

When the early *Āryan-s*, in the native joy of their care free life in luxurious circumstances, reached the Gangetic plains, the beauty spot of the world, they got intoxicated, as it were, with the very goodness of life. Life was kind to them; the rich happiness and the healthy love that they come to enjoy in the era made their life a colourful song. As children of God they revelled in the lap of *Gaṅgā* where they knew not what sorrow was, since they were not under the persecutions of any disturbing desires within, any insulting privations of life without. The virgin soil, at times, yielded crops even 200-fold practically without any effort at all.

Salubrious climate, majestic forests, glorious rivers, magnanimous mountains; the bright blue dome, the roaring oceans, the beautiful nights and the happy contented communal living... these early fore-fathers of the *Hindū* tradition found themselves placed in a wondrous atmosphere well-suited for poetry and growth. In their leisure moments they did not sit in idleness to listen to the hissing of the serpents and did not try to taste the forbidden, but on the contrary stretched themselves down in the embracing warmth of the shade and spent their leisure hours in the gorgeous avenues of delightful poetry and pulsating songs. They expressed their wondrous inspiration at the throbbing beauty... that lay splashed in its luxurious extravagance around and about them, far and near, up above in the skies and down below on the plains.

Sheltered thus in a world amidst the tapestry of forests and rivers, when they rested on the soft carpets of the all-giving earth under an ever changing canopy of magical colours, they basked in the tropical sun and almost unknowingly burst themselves into irresistible poetry, adoring the beauty that constantly played a game of hide-and-seek all around them. The early *Āryan-s* sang the song of their joy addressing the rivers and the trees, the mountains and the clouds, the sun and the moon, the rain and the wind, the fields and the rivers, man and animals. Such praises together constitute the earliest religion of that era and they are handed down to us intact in the *Mantra* portion of the *Vedā-s*.

Soon they multiplied in numbers. The pressure of population on land slowly increased. Climate became more a nd more undependable and, therefore, the agricultural folk who peopled the Gangetic valley felt the need of some Father in the Heaven who will kindly protect them from the inclemencies of the weather, and guard them against their sorrows and tragedies in their domestic and social life. Instinctively they turned towards these phenomenal factors themselves and thus conceived of a Fire-God, an Ocean-God, a Tree-God, a River- god, a Rain-God, etc., and started propitiating them through prayer, worship and ritualism. The instructions for such ritualistic worship are found in the *Brāhmaṇa* portion of the *Vedā-s*.

Society still progressed and came to a stage when the ritualism became more and more complicated, and though it served the ordinary folk and gave them the intellectual poise and mental tranquillity to face the threatening challenge of life with hope and faith, there was a group of highly intellectual and eminent men who were impatient with the *Brāhmaṇa* portion and strove hard to discover a more satisfactory path of Truth. Their contemplation and philosophical quest brought them to the discovery that godliness is not "there yonder," but "here within" themselves. The enunciations of this theory and the description of the technique by which the Divine in us can be experienced are constituted in the *Upaniṣadik* portion of the *Vedā-s*.

The *Mantrā-s*, the *Brāhmaṇā-s* and the *Upaniṣad-s* were all memorised by the students from their teachers, and the later generations of disciples learned them from their elders. As each generation got the heritage from the elders at each period, new details, clarifying and describing the same fundamental Truth, were added to it, in their discourses. Of course, the text remained the same, but the explanations were always original.

The entire *Vedik* literature was handed down by the *Gurū-s* to their disciples by word of mouth, and the students had to preserve them in memory. The scheme worked well so long as the pre-occupation of living was not too severe; but as the population increased, the competition in life also became keener and man had to wage his battle of life on almost all his sphere of activity. Accommodation, land, cultivation, harvesting, transporting, storing, etc., all became more and more a burden upon man's mental life. Over-burdened with these, he became unsteady in his intellectual poise and proved incapable of memorising the voluminous literature and reproducing them faithfully.

Hindūism was facing then the danger of a total annihilation. Scripture was fast fading away even from among those who were supposed to be the custodians of the sacred lore. It is at such a crucial juncture in our spiritual history that we find the advent of the great revolutionary reformer, the poet-philosopher, *Vyāsa*. He, the son of a *brāhmaṇa*—*Parāśara*—born of a fisher-woman, *matsyāgandhi*, had in his make up the instinctive daring of a fisherman, and the acquired nobility and self-discipline of a *brāhmaṇa*. Both these he brought into his work.

With the daring of a fisherman he was able to face the opposition of the orthodoxy; with his mother's in-born capacity...to see through the mountainous waves of the sea and perceive the living world of fishes that people the serene depths of the ocean....he retrieved the life-giving gems of wisdom that lay almost unnoticed in the bowels of the then existing social confusions and life's commotions. He collected the *Vedik* passages and for the first time edited them into four written volumes which constitute today the four great *Vedā-s* of the *Hindū-s*: the *Ṛg Veda*, the *Yajur Veda*, the *Sāma Veda* and the *Atharvaṇa Veda*. Each book contains three sections; the *Mantra* portion, the *Brāhmaṇa* Section and the *Upaniṣad-s*. The *Upaniṣad*-s, thus, are all found in the last section of each *Veda* and, therefore, the philosophy of the *Upaniṣad*-s had come to be otherwise called as *Vedānta*...the end of *Veda*.

Any intelligent reader of scientific temperament, if he were to read these three, with some understanding, can easily perceive that a healthy creative revolt against *Mantrā-s* gave birth to the *Brāhmaṇā-s*, the ritualistic portion, which in its own maturity put forth the glories of the *Upaniṣad-s*. The relative positions of these three sections on the scales of the human growth can be easily compared with the birth and growth of a flower and its fulfilment in its fruit.

The peeping buds represent the *mantrā-s*; the blushing petals in all their glory of colour, fragrance and joy dancing in the passing breeze and continuously courted by the murmuring bees, represent the *Brāhmaṇa* portion where desire-laden courtiers enter to invoke the Gods to gain more and more for their prosperous cells. In their own maturity the colours fade away, the petals shrink and they ultimately fall down dancing in the air in the ecstasy of their sense of fulfilment. They are sure that where they stood, the fruit shall come to flourish. The fruit in its unripe stage during its formation may be compared with the *Āraṇyakā-s* which constitute the transitional period that must necessarily intervene between the extrovert seeking and the introvert discovery, and when the fruit is mature and ready to fall down... capable of giving birth to many a mother plant which shall in their turn, produce hundreds of flowers and each flower in its turn may produce scrores of seeds, ...it represents the extremely creative, virulently potent, uncompromisingly dynamic philosophy of the *Upaniṣad-s*.

On a general view of the total contents of the *Vedā-s*, we can easily find that the earlier portions of *mantrā-s* are the description of the Truth perceived by the poets through the trellis of the names-and-forms that clothe Mother Nautre's beauty; the *Brāhmaṇā-s* constitute the description of the same Eternal Truth seen through the intricate intellectual machinery of the priest, and the *Upaniṣad-s* constitute the declarations of the Philosophers who have crawled along the precipitous sides of mellow wisdom to reach the pinnacles of brilliant experiences of the Eternal and the Perfect. In short, the poet, the priest and the philosopher, all gazing at the effulgence of the same spiritual Truth that lie concealed behind the jungles of the body, mind and intellect have sung in their own language the ecstatic song of wonderment and voiceless inspiration which were remembered by our forefathers. These memorised flakes or sparkling wisdom treasured and handed down to us is the sacred heritage of the *Hindū* culture compiled and preserved to-day in the volumes called the *Vedā-s*.

The theme of the *Vedā-s*, therefore, is the Infinite and the Eternal. It described the realm that lies beyond the worlds that are known to us, perceived and experienced through the gross equipments of our body, mind and intellect. Beyond the purview of the waking, dream and deep-sleep states, lies stretched, the soft world of bliss and beatitude where the finite mortal rediscovers himself to be of the stature of God, the Infinite. Necessarily, therefore, the language of the market place, the words of the drawing-room, the phrases of the slums, the slang of drinking booth, can never hope to express the Perfect and the Immortal. Language cannot define, cannot even vaguely report upon the transcendental experience which one comes to live in the stillness of one's own mind. *To define Truth*, therefore, *is to defile Truth.*

Language is constituted of a series of words arranged in a scientific order and each word is a sound symbol that can create in the mind of the hearer a definite pattern of thought invoking a similar experience. These symbols of sound representing definite experiences are all pre-determined in a society and therefore, we can transact through language only such experiences which are common to all in that society. Thus when I say "Sweet as honey" my hearers can definitely understand what I mean, because sweetness of honey is a common experience in the bosom of all, but if I were to say, "as stiff as Vodka," my Indian friends shall fail to understand, while our Russian comrades may exactly understand what I mean; the drink Vodka is not experienced by Indians although this drink is familiar to the Russian brothers.

With this in mind when we try to estimate the effect of words in expressing the transcendental, we understand that the style in all the scriptures of the world must be peculiar. The words are used in the scripture not merely in their ordinary connotations but also mainly in their flavour-contents of suggestiveness.

Because the words are employed in their suggestiveness, a student who has but a grammar knowledge of *Saṁskṛta*, when he dashes into the portals of the *Upaniṣad-s*, gets himself confounded at a staggering nonsense that the words in their dictionary meaning seem to bark out; at the same time these students, vain in their erudition and scholarship, fail to find in themselves the courage to admit their incapacity and thus without seeking for a Master they learn the text and commentaries mechanically by heart and trot the countries as Olympus striding in His wisdom without doing any service to mankind or to themselves but only leaving fantastic foot prints upon the face of Mother Earth.

In our daily transaction of language we are apt to exaggerate the capacity of the words, and in modern times we have almost the feeling that there can be nothing which we can experience but cannot express. This is only an exaggerated faith in language; almost a superstition. Scientifically analysed, we can discover the limitations of words, although in themselves, for all our day-to-day practical purposes, they are mighty and almost all-powerful. Words can be employed, the *Ṛṣī-s* have discovered, only in expressing *four types of meaning*; beyond these, words are helpless sounds:

1. They can describe the substance (*Vaśtu*),

2. They can describe the properties (*guṇā-s*),

3. They can describe vividly all the activities (*kriyā*) and also

4. They describe and exactly point out the innumerable shades of the relationship that exist among the finite things of the world (*sambandha*).

Beyond these four-fold capacities, words cannot express anything at all and, in fact these four together constitute the entire world of finite things. But if there is a Truth or a factor that can fall into no definite species, has no qualities, in itself has no action and maintains no relationship with anything else in the world, certainly that Truth cannot be expressed by gross finite words of any language in the world.

The theme of the *Ṛṣī-s* was the transcendental Truth which is not a perishable commodity (*Vastu*), which is without *guṇa* without *kriyā* and without *sambandha*, and therefore, in dealing with this All-pervading Truth, the one-without-a-second, they had to first of all, prepare a special language which had a greater share of indicative wealth than any other language in the world. A language so prepared for this purpose, cultured (*saṁskṛta*) to roar the inexpressible is the language called *Saṁskṛta.*

In the *Vedā-s* Truth is not described. It is only indicated. A subtle head that can follow the extremely scientific arguments and a flowing heart with sympathetic love ringing in unison with the bosom of the Master when fired up with faith, devotion, earnestness, sincerity and goodwill alone can appreciate and understand *Vedānta,* and ultimately come to experience the glory of the Divine Reality behind the seeming sorrows and apparent imperfection of the world.

Hence the need for a seeker to be at the feet of a sympathetic Master who lives the Perfection, not only in his mouth but with every movement of his breath.

Unfortunately we, today, find this tradition ripped open and molested even in the sacred hermitages of modern *āśramā-s* that trade behind the sacred name of the immortal culture. Such black-marketeers in religion do hasten the decadence of *Hindūism* rather than help to revive and bring about the much needed renaissance in India. Sure enough, when the rising tide of renascent *Hindūism* reaches them, only a miracle can save their institutions and their propped-up and bloated grace and glory!

Our text-book *Aitareya Upaniṣad* belongs to the *Brāhmaṇa* portion of the *Ṛg Veda.* It is constituted of six sections* and therefore, *Śaṅkara* calls it '*Ātma Ṣaṭka.*' The author of the *Aitareya Upaniṣad* is definitely known; but as a matter of fact the *Upaniṣad-s* are without the signatures of their authors. At rare instances, however, due to internal evidence, we get an inkling of who gave a particular *Upaniṣad* for the first time to the world of seekers. Thus *Yājñavalkya* of

---

* Prima facie there are only five sections in this *Upaniṣad*—three in Ch. I, and one each in Ch. II and III. *Śaṅkara* considers the Peace Invocation (*Śānti-Pāṭha*) passage as one independent Section..... Ed.

Bṛhadāraṇyaka Upaniṣad, Lord Death of *Kaṭhopaniṣad*, *Bhagavān Pippalāda* of *Praśna Upaniṣad*, are all exceptional cases where we happen to know at least what was the name of the *Guru-Ṛṣi*.

Self-effacement is the secret of inspiration; a genius at work is he who has established a perfect identity of his own mind and intellect with the work in hand. The best can come out of an orator or a painter or a sculptor or a musician or a writer only when he forgets himself and gets lost in the work in hand.

Similarly, the Masters having transcended their ego-centric existence perfectly merged in the Supreme when they murmured their voiceless ecstasy through their broken, fumbled words from the peaks of their realised and lived perfections; you and I, belonging to the disciple class, can but receive a whiff of the ethereal joy through these words. When the Master gets awakened to the consciousness of the body and mind, he darés not claim his own 'truth' declarations as his own for he has to, with his mind and intellect, re-digest his own words, as it were, to enjoy intellectually what he lived intuitively.

Yet luckily for us, there is a beautiful story through which the tradition gives us some idea of the identity of the Master behind this wonder-scripture.

Tradition attributes the *Aitareya Brāhmaṇa*[1] to a seer called *Mahidāsa* who was the son of *a brāhmaṇa*[2] named *Viśāla* born to his mother *Itarā*. When the boy grew up to the age of five, one day when his father was sitting near the '*Homa Kuṇḍa*' as an *Yajamāna*, the boy wanted to go and sit on the lap of his father.

As the boy was his son through his 'other' (*itarā*) wife, the boy was not allowed this privilege. The dejected child

1. Ritualistic portion of the *Vedā-s*.
2. One of the four *Varṇā-s*.

sobbing, came to his mother and reported the sad incident in his melodious blabbering language. The motherly heart of *Itarā* burnt with anger, and smouldered at the thought that it was her weakness that had brought this insult upon her innocent child; she fell on the ground and embraced her *Iṣṭa Devatā*, Mother earth.

Mother India manifested herself to bless her devotee, and at the request of *Itarā* the spirit of *Hindūism* initiated *Mahidāsa* (servant of the earth) into the great wisdom, the secret of our immortal culture. The boy grew perfect and came to declare to the world in his own language....the language of the low and discarded, the language of the worker, of the slave, in the language of the common man... the infinite theme of Perfection and how man can come to experience his Godhood in himself...which we know is the vital core of our culture.

The above story should elicit more sympathy from our present generation as it is evidently clear that *Itarā's* son (*Aitareya*) was not a *brāhmaṇa* by birth and that his name was *Mahidāsa* (earth-slave; the son of the soil). Again, it is evident that *Itarā's Iṣṭa Devatā* was Mother Earth. Can it be that she belonged to the potter community? Anyway that she was not a *brāhmaṇa* is clear from the word '*Itarā*' meaning 'the other.'

In this story you and I need not read the social injustice of that period, as we have no other evidence to prove similar injustice although in our present period of *Hindū* decadence we are finding a million such instances. It would be healthy for us to understand that in the mysticism of the story lies concealed a more profitable truth. A *brāhmaṇa* seed, *sāttvik* to the core, when reinforced with the perseverance and industry of an artisan, who is ready to sweat and toil to eke out even a little of comfort and happiness, is the fit instrument to walk diligently up the mighty Path of Knowledge to the Eternal sunlit-Peaks of the *Vedāntik* Realisation and Perfect Godhood. Again, however low born one may be...and according to *Sanātana Dharma*, every body is born a *śudra*....by dint of self perseverance and daring courage in seeking, one can raise oneself culturally to the eminence of the perfection which is pointed out in the *Upaniṣad* and which is gained by the true *brāhmaṇa*, one who realised *Brahman*.

Therefore, friends, we must be ready, while reading this *Upaniṣad*, to meet with similies and metaphors taken from a potter's life and to that extent we may say that *Aitareya Upaniṣad* is the Scripture of the Common-man, the Bible of the proletarian, the Quoran of the Labourer! God-hood attained by a son of the soil is our *Aitareya*, and the *Upaniṣad* is the song of our *Hindū* culture from a hut of the 'slum.'

This great *Upaniṣad* consisting of six sections*, otherwise called the "*Ātma Ṣaṭka*," tries to indicate the Eternal Principle, in and through its manifestations, by the familiar method of super-imposition and negation' technically called in *Saṁskṛta* as the *Āropa* and *Apavāda*. The technique is the same as that which we follow in pigmenting the slides of a microscope before our observations. In trying to observe and study the size, shade and arrangement of the cells in a particular specimen of observation, the slide is generally pigmented by some colouring material, so that the margins of the cells may clearly be traced out for the observer. The observer, though he sees the colour, understands it only as a convenience which he has deliberately thrown upon the specimen for the purpose of efficient observation and study.

Similarly, in the *Upaniṣad-s*, in almost all the elaborate theories of Creation described from time to time, the main aim of the Master was to superimpose the creation upon the Truth and later on, through a total negation (*Apavāda*) of it, to indicate its substratum, the Truth. When the *ghost* has been

---

* We have already pointed out elsewhere that *Śaṅkara* counts Peace Invocation passage at the end as an independent section to make a *'Ṣaṭka'* (i.e., six)---Ed.

seen, the deluded person cannot have at the same time even a vague perception of the '*post*' behind; when the *ghost* has been negated the '*post*' becomes easily evident and quite clear.

Some of our friends in the West, who with a slight study of *Saṁskṛta* boast themselves to be students of the Wisdom of the East, have made honest efforts to understand the immortal '*Upaniṣadik*' lore of the *Hindū-s*. At the end of it all, they have come to feel a despairing sense of confusion and have cried out their despair in their wise-looking declarations that intuition is not a dependable instrument of knowledge, since the *Ṛṣī-s* of India have not been able to give one unanimous theory for the Creation of the world. They find as many as some thirty different Theories of Creation propounded by the various Masters in the '*Upaniṣadik*' literature; and when there is more than one description of the same object from two different observers, then their instruments of perception must be different. Some western critics, therefore, have chosen to under-estimate the reliability of the power of intuition, the *Jñāna*-vision.

When a physicist, a poet, a musician and a dull-witted fool, all sleep, we know that in dreamless-sleep the experience of all is the same joy; and yet, when they wake up and try to report and explain their experience, each will explain differently. And, to any sincere student it will be clear on a closer analysis that, though their words are different, the indicated joy-of-sleep is the same.

So too, these Masters transcending, through the process of meditation, their body-mind-intellect-world consciousness, come to live the Bliss of Pure Awareness; at that moment of God-consciousness, to them there is only the Greater and the Diviner Life Eternal. When they, later on, come down to the body-level then alone they try to explain; naturally, their intellectual interpretation must be different from Seer to Seer, from prophet to prophet, from Sage to Sage.....and the differences in their descriptions are the differences of the texture of their intellectual capacities and previous mental habits of thought.

Again, the teachers were not at all anxious to give to the world a Theory of Creation, for they had experienced that the multiple world of objects-emotions-ideas is a distortion of Truth produced when Consciousness gets deflected while passing through the prism of body-mind-intellect. Their's was the anxiety to help the anxious disciples that had reached them with a firm faith in the reality of life as perceived by them, and were seeking only a remedy for the choking sense of finitude that they were experiencing in life. To declare to them, the Truth that in the Infinite, the finite has no existence, would be to frighten them away; the *Ṛṣī-s* wanted to cure the mis-understanding of the seekers rather than pulverise their spirit of enquiry by revelations too staggering to console or to revive.

Thus the *Ṛṣī-s* carefully studied each student and according to the type that reached them, they gave an analytical enumeration or a synthetic theory of how from the Infinite-Eternal-Reality, the finite world of perceptions rose up. Each explanation has a false charm which can satisfy the restlessness of a particular type of student. When the student is thus harboured in a seeming phase of satisfying inner peace... from his own agitating doubts regarding the '*how*' of the Creation...the Seers treat their disciples for a greater and permanent cure.

These Theories of Creation have an intrinsic capacity in them, not only to lull the suffocating restlessness of the questioning intellect but they open up a thousand new vistas of original thought, which, left to themselves, they would never have come upon to explore.

In every theory there are one or two (sometimes even more) inconsistencies or 'missing links' which are so beautifully clothed in the melodious beauty of the mellifluous wings of the music of the passages, never suspect them.

Later on the Sages took up their discourses and allowing their disciples to follow them close at their heels, conducted them up the mountains, down the dales, and along the waters'edge in the landscape of philosophy, and as an efficient guide brought them suddenly out of the confusing jungles of intellectualism into the open fields of the Spiritual Truth. On reaching there, the students discover for themselves the fallacy of their own doubts, the meaningless-ness of their problems and academic questions, the purposeless-ness of their intellectual quests which they sought so far.

The teacher, in this fulfilment, looks with joy into the sparkling eyes of their students; the grateful eyes of the students look into the serener depths of the teacher's truthful eyes: both come to understand each other. The teacher's look plead. "what can I do? I had to charm you with an elaborate story of Creation," the students' looks gratefully accepted, "yes, we do realise how foolish were our doubts and how you were compelled to treat our stupidity with such a severe antidote in the form of a fable!"

Peace Invocation

(*Śāntipāṭhaḥ*)

ॐ वाङ् मे मनसि प्रतिष्ठिता
मनो मे वाचि प्रतिष्ठितमाविरावीर्म एधि ।
वेदस्य म आणीस्थः श्रुतं मे मा प्रहासीः ।
अनेनाधीतेनाहोरात्रान् सन्दधामि ऋतं वदिष्यामि ।
सत्यं वदिष्यामि । तन्मामवतु । तद्वक्तारमवतु ।
अवतु मामवतु वक्तारमवतु वक्तारम् ।।
ॐ शान्तिः ! शान्तिः !! शान्तिः !!!

Oṁ vāṅ me manasi pratiṣṭhitā,
mano me vāci pratiṣṭhitam-āvirā-vīrma edhi,
vedasya ma āṇīsthaḥ śrutaṁ me mā prahāsīḥ,
anenā-dhītenā-horātrān sanda-dhāmi ṛtaṁ vadiṣyāmi,
satyaṁ vadiṣyāmi, tanmām-avatu, tad-vaktāram-avatu,
avatu mām-avatu vaktāram-avatu vaktāram.

Oṁ śāntiḥ, śāntiḥ, śāntiḥ.

ॐ वाङ् *Oṁ vāṅ* = speech; मे *me* = my; मनसि *manasi* = in mind; प्रतिष्ठिता *pratiṣṭhitā* = be rooted; मनः *manaḥ* = mind; मे *me* = my; वाचि *vāci* = in speech; प्रतिष्ठितम् *pratiṣṭhitam* = is rooted; आविर आवीर मे एधि *āvir āvīr me edhi* = *Brahman* reveal thyself to me; वेदस्य *vedasya* = of the *Veda* theme; मे आणीस्थः *me āṇīsthaḥ* = may I master; श्रुतम् *śrutam* = that (I have) heard; मे *me* = me; मा *mā* = do not; प्रहासीः *prahāsīḥ* = forsake; अनेन *anena* = by this; अधीतेन *adhītena* = by studies; अहोरात्रान् *ahorātrān* = days and nights; सन्दधामि *sandadhāmi* = continuously live; ऋतम् *ṛtam* =

truth; वदिष्यामि *vadiṣyāmi* = think (speak); सत्यम् *satyam* = truth; वदिष्यामि *vadiṣyāmi* = will speak; तत् *tat* = that (truth); माम् *mām* = me; अवतु *avatu* = protect; तत् *tat* = that (truth); वक्तारम् *vaktāram* = he, who speaks (teacher); अवतु *avatu* = protect; माम् अवतु *avatu mām* = protect me; अवतु *avatu* = protect; वक्तारम् *vaktāram* = teacher; अवतु वक्तारम् *avatu vaktāram.*= protect the teacher.

ॐ शान्तिः *Oṁ śāntiḥ* = peace be; शान्तिः *śāntiḥ* = peace be; शान्तिः *śāntiḥ* = peace be.

Peace Invocation

Oṁ! *May my speech be rooted in my mind, may my mind be rooted in my speech;* Brahman, *reveal Thyself to me. Oh! Mind and speech, enable me to grasp the Truth that the* Vedā-s *teach. Let not what I have heard forsake me. Let me continuously live my days and nights in my studies. I think truth; I speak truth. May that (truth) protect me. May that protect the teacher; protect me; protect the teacher; protect the teacher!!*

Oṁ! Peace, Peace, Peace.

Before the actual study of the *Upaniṣad-s* is undertaken, the students used to assemble for the purpose, at the feet of the Master and used to chant along with the teacher a chorus song addressed to Truth, invoking the grace of the Supreme, so that there may be a continuous unison established between the teacher and the taught throughout the study-session.

This vividly shows that the *Āryan Ṛṣī-s* even in the hermitages near the Ganges banks while initiating the students to the secrets of the Pure *Advaitik* Truth, were not against the principle of *Bhakti* or the practice of prayer. The idea that prayer, through surrender and love, at the Supreme is against the canons of *Vedānta,* is a clamour of a very recent origin only propounded by shameless demogorgons who are, erudite scholars no doubt, but not sincere seekers or realised Men of Perfection.

Though the *Ṛṣī-s* had recognised the efficiency of prayer as a technique of self-development, they did not conceive the ugly practices of prayer which are now the accepted routine in our temples and other houses-of-god indulged in the name of *Bhakti*. What we are now witnessing is a miserable travesty of the Truth of the scriptures, mis-handled and distorted by self-seeking commentators and scheming intellects who have their own purposes and plans to loot the ignorant but credulous public. Indeed, the cheap practices of bribing God is a corruption of the Science of Religion, which can bless none but the temple institutions and their trustees, and can bring, alas! only a positive destruction of the very moral integrity of the devotees.

Rare and subtle adjustments in our mind by which it gets tuned up to the higher inspirations of the Divine, through thrilling devotion or scintillating intellectualism constitute the enduring technique of prayer. There is, in true prayers, no attempt on the part of the devotee to coax or force, to persuade or to compel, to purchase or to canvas the Supreme for His grace. In the scriptural text-books we find but a peaceful and dignified self-approximation of the devotee towards the absolute concept of the Eternal and the Divine; and this is considered as true prayer.

This peace invocation is typical of the intellectual integrity of the *Upaniṣadik* age when the students knew the deeper psychology of right living and high thinking, and we find that in this short chorus song a wealth of practical psychology is hinted at, in simple quick strokes.

The opening line is a prayer unto the Supreme coming from the heart of a seeker, who cries for the Divine grace, so that he may come to live easily with his words faithfully wedded to his mind; also, he wants his mind always to be truly and fully expressed in the fragrance of his words. Unless we are ready to express what we sincerely feel in ourselves we will be untrue to ourselves, and the path that leads to the flowery gardens of Truth is not paved with untruths; darkness, however intense it may be, cannot produce light!!

Again, all the great Masters of the world have constantly advised seekers to maintain a perfect consistency between their thoughts and expressions. If this is not practised properly, the student will never be able to express his spiritual doubts correctly and precisely to the teacher. Moreover, if an individual lives a life of disintegration in which his words express something different from what his mind declares, there will be a dangerous shattering in his inner personality. A cracked instrument cannot bring forth its full music when the strings are played upon by the flying fingers of inspiration of any artist.

In many of the passages of the *Upaniṣad-s* we detect such simple strokes which portent the volume of true knowledge in psychology that was available to the *Ṛṣī-s* in those days. Compared with this wealth of knowledge that was popular then, the modern text books of psychology read as elementary and imperfect to the core. The *Vedik* student and teachers seems to have realised fully well that through long practices in self-inconsistencies we develop a forked-personality, each fact neutralising and cancelling the efficiency of the other!! Therefore, they prayed for inner strength to live every moment of their lives in healthy harmony between their mental waves and verbal expressions.

Brahman, give thyself to me:—Students who have got themselves established in a healthy way of living gain necessary qualifications in their head and heart; and they can start the study of the scriptures at the feet of a Master. Naturally, the students demand the Supreme Goal to reveal Itself to them. The Self-confidence that arises out of a Life Divine lived can give us a love-right to demand even the highest fruit directly from the Supreme.

When we have tuned our radio receiving-set in our drawing room and when we are quite confident that we have tuned it properly, we can, in our expectations, demand to hear clearly the programme relayed by the broadcasting station to which we have set our instrument. Similarly, when the student has thus lived in the grosser honesty—a consistency between thought and speech—he comes to feel that *Brahman* must reveal to him, since it is his birth right to realise the Infinite and the Eternal.

In the *Hindū* scriptures *Brahman* is the term that indicates the Supreme Reality which is All-pervading and whose manifestations are the entire world of the living—the Eternal Substratum, changeless and infinite; the source of all activity and knowledge. *Ātman* is a term used to indicate the 'touch of life' in the seeker which is available for his direct realisation. At the moment of experiencing the *ātman*, the individual experiences at once the non-dual *Brahman*. The outer infinite space is in no way different from, and is certainly one with, the cup-space.

The students and the teacher assemble together to teach and learn the scriptural declarations given out by the *Ṛṣī-s* of old. Unlike other text-books, the scriptures can best be understood and fully reacted with only when they are delivered by a man of experience and purity, of sincerity and fire. Therefore, the disciples at the feet of the Master renounce all other activities and bring to a single-pointedness all their sense-organs; and the only instruments that are brought to function diligently in the study of *Vedānta* are the sense of hearing to listen to the words spoken by the teacher and the mind of the student. The words of the Master must convey the shock of his spiritual 'charge.' When these words, rising from his bosom and revelling in the Infinite experience, enter in through the ears of the student, they reach the vigilant but peaceful, alert but passionless, dynamic but not restless minds of the disciples. They can then create in the listener's mind the exact waves of experiences as the Master feels during his discourse. This idea is very well brought out in the passage now under discussion.

The student, addressing the deities of Speech and Mind, requests them to enable him to grasp the Truth that the *Vedā-s* declares.

Let what I have heard slip not from me:—Vedānta being a complete and perfect Science of Living, each day's lesson has a direct bearing upon the arguments and explanations that the teacher will be giving on the following day. The continuity of study can be fruitfully maintained only when the student has not only a capacity for a quick grasping, but also a diligent memory in which what has been grasped once be distinctly preserved as the carvings on granite pillars! This capacity, generally termed in *Saṁskṛta* as *"Medhāśakti,"* is an important item in the inner wealth of a true seeker on the Path of Knowledge.

May I join day with night in study:—The above mentioned capacity for remembering all the previous discourses is acquired through a self-conscious and deliberate effort on the part of the student. It is not by the accidental grace received by some, and not gained by others, that one is capable of reacting well but not remembering the whole, while another student comes to remember all that he has learnt. Memory is facilitated by continuously employing the mind to dwell upon those thoughts for a long period, and this mental and intellectual process of assimilation of what we have heard is called 'reflection' (*manan*).

To do *Manan,* we need not renounce the world or run away into a quiet corner. It is most effectively undertaken by maintaining in one corner of the mind these thoughts to smoulder. A small quantity of incense burning at one end of a hall can impart its fragrance throughout the hall, and even waft the same sweetness to the atmosphere outside the windows. So too, the *Vedāntik* discourse heard once may be allowed to smoulder at one end of the mind and it will soon spread its fragrance into the wider world of one's own thoughts and ideas within and speech and actions without.

This process is to be undertaken studiously and sincerely at least in the early days of our studies, all through the day and night, and this idea is indicated in this passage. On the whole, it means that since I am striving consciously to get fully integrated by deliberately avoiding all disintegrating tendencies in myself... since I faithfully listen to and carefully react with the words of my master... since I continuously reflect upon these truths days and nights, I have every right to demand of the

Supreme to "reveal Thyself to me." For, the *Vedāntik* path of Self-realisation consists of hearing and reflecting upon that which is heard with a full concentration, which can come only out of a personality that is not at all shattered.

I think truth, I speak truth:—We have been, from childhood onwards, hearing that we should be truthful and honest and that untruth and falsehood will bring upon us sorrows and despairs. Such ethical laws can have no hold upon a generation that is extremely scientific, grossly intellectual. We can respect and faithfully follow such instructions only when we are initiated into the logic of such advices. Gone are the puritanic days of the middle ages or the reverential era of blind obedience, or the age of unquestioning loyalty of the patriarchal society. To-day even a child instinctively questions every ethical rule and moral injunction. Obedience to these laws becomes implicit the moment we are able to make our generation see the rationale behind such moral insistence.

"*I think truth (Ṛtam)*" means, my intellect is soaked with the studies of the scripture which explain to me the Absolute Truth and the ideal way of true living. Thus, I patiently educate my intellect on the lines of the text-book and come to a certain intellectual culture which is dependable and pleasing to myself and to others.

Having thus digested properly and assimilated the truths of life, I allow my intellect to grow in them into a healthy stature which has its own ideals and idealisms. Having gained this poise, thereafter I train my mind always to think in terms of my own intellectual convictions. And then "*I speak the truth*" meaning, thereafter I express by my word of mouth truly what I think.

These expressions thus indicate a highly dynamic inner life wherein the educated intellect is trained to be always on the alert and be ever vigilant at the top windows of its own towers, constantly policing the mind. The mind is disciplined to give an unquestioning fidelity to the intellect. When the mind thinks in unison with the intellect, those thoughts are faithfully echoed through words; and the intellect is all-along on the watch over the words.

When, thus, this triple-stringed instrument of speech, mind and intellect is perfectly tuned up to sing in concord, the resonanace of melody that rises from it, is the true song of salutations and adoration to the Divine, housed in the temple of one's own body.

Since the seeker is thus constantly making his very life a prayerful song unto the Lord in him, he has every right to demand that the Spirit should protect him and his Master. For the purposes of emphasis is the repetition, "*protect me, protect the teacher.*" The repetition "*protect the teacher*" at the end of the passage is to indicate the conclusion of the section; this *Upaniṣad* is called "*Ātma Ṣaṭka*" only when we consider this peace invocation passage as one of it sections.

After this brilliant prayer both the teacher and the taught sing together, "*Peace, Peace, Peace.*" The thrice-repeated prayer for peace is not merely an idle extravagance in words but they fulfil a definite purpose. Many obstacles may come to blast our chance for hearing continuously the brilliant discourse of a teacher roaring in the hours of his inspiration. All the possible obstacles have been carefully classified under three main headings by the acutely analytical intellect of the *Ṛṣī-s*. They classified all possible obstacles under three headings with reference to the sources from which these obstacles arise.

The three groups into which all the probable obstacles in the study of the scriptures can fall are:—(a) God-sent (*Ādhi-daivika*), such as lightning, thunder, etc.; (b) phenomenal (*Ādhi-bhautika*), such as fire, floods, landslide, tigers, hooligans, etc.; (c) purely subjective (*Adhyātmika)* such as inertia, lack of faith, insincerity, and such other negativities that arise from within us and break up the healthy unison between the teacher and the taught.

This peace-chanting is sung both by the teacher and the taught every day at the beginning and close of their lessons. After establishing this desirable unison between them, the text starts.

Chapter I

Section i - प्रथम खण्ड

ॐ आत्मा वा इदमेक एवाग्र आसीत् ।
नान्यत् किंचन मिषत् ।

Oṁ ātmā vā idameka evāgra āsīt,
nānyat kiñcana miṣat.

ॐ *oṁ* = *Oṁ*; आत्मा *ātmā* = *ātmā* (Self); वा *vā* = verily; इदम् *idam* = this; एक *eka* = one; एव *eva* = only; अग्र *agra* = in the beginning; आसीत् *āsīt* = was; न *na* = not; अन्यत् *anyat* = other; किञ्चन *kiñcana* = anything; मिषत् *miṣat* = winking.

1a. *In the beginning, verily,* Ātman *(Self) alone was this (the Universe)...nothing else active whatsoever...*

In the peace-invocation passage, the teacher and the taught had each reminded the other of the great and noble values of the Life Divine that are to be strictly followed, so that in the shattering contact with the world outside the seeker may not get disintegrated within himself. They together prayed for the grace of the Supreme and demanded the revelation of *Brahman* within them.

After this common prayer at the altars of the Self, they enter into the text-book proper in which a scientific enquiry is made into the Nature and contents of the perceived world for the purpose of understanding the real substratum for this world of finitude.

It is a well-known fact that change can take place only upon a changeless ground; the moving train must have rigid and solidly fixed rails; the moving waters of the river must have a motionless river-bed. Constant change can be maintained only upon a changeless substratum. The ever-changing variety of light and shade that are projected in a film-theatre can give us the enchanting illusion of a continuous story only when they fall upon steady and motionless screen, spotlessly clean.

Similarly, the world, as available to us, is everchanging and the continuity of change itself gives us the illusion of the relative permanency of the world. For this phenomena of continuous change, we must have a changeless, permanent factor, and the scriptural text-books are all essentially an enquiry into the existence and nature of this Absolute Factor.

Upaniṣad-s are all a discussion upon the Reality, that took place between the teacher and the student, in the melodious quietude of the Ganges banks, deep in the sequestered valleys of the *Himālayā-s*. A diligent seeker approaches the Master who is always a man full of his experience of the Divine. The seeker is made to live in close association with the teacher for a sufficiently long period, until they are knit together by indissoluble bonds of mutual love and respect, admiration and reverence, consideration and regard. Then and then alone, do the teacher and the taught sit together for the purpose of discussing the subtler and the divine substratum of the manifested life.

The student had approached the Master some time back, and during the first meeting, the boy's mind was full of queries upon the nature of life, and the goal of existence. He had tried to intelligently grasp the purpose of life through an objective observation of the things and beings, happenings and the circumstances, situations and conditions of life, as were available to him through his perceptions.

"From where did all these come? Why have they come? When did the Creation first start? How! Why? When? What was there before the Creation?" .... in breathless excitement the boy poured out his intellectual confusions, emotional surprises, sentimental wonderment and loving anxieties in an impulsive outflow of tumbling emotion. Those questions were not directly and immediately answered by the teacher.

Later on, the student was disciplined slowly and steadily, until at last when both the teacher and the taught were fully tuned up with each other, when their hearts have become moulded into one, then alone did the transaction of knowledge actually start in all seriousness. The scriptural discourses start, therefore, with the answering of may questions the student had, while approaching the Master.

The *Upaniṣad-s* become almost flavourless and at times, even meaningless, if we ever forget to read these passages without reference to the background of the teacher and the taught. As it, were, we may say that each page in the scripture is printed on paper that carries the design of a hermitage at the *verāṇḍā* of which sits an anxious teacher, glowing with his inspiration while talking to a student who, in his turn, is sitting physically dumb, in his love and respect for the Master, and yet, extremely alert in his mind and intellect. Every word or passage that comes from the Master is attentively heard and the student is studiously examining it at the touch-stone of his own intellectual understanding.

Whenever the student cannot appreciate or follow closely any argument given out by the Master, he is not at all shy to express on his brilliant face his confusion, and the Master who is continuously observing the face and the eyes of the student will not leave even the slightest suspicion of a doubt in the student unsolved. At every little doubt which the boy may express, the Master will, with divine charity and Godly love, pause and elaborate upon until the difficulty is removed totally, entirely.

Together they go stage by stage, walking up the sides of the mountain of Olympus, precipitous and risky, and whenever the *Ṛṣi* finds the panting youngster trembling at the edges, he would lend him his hand and help him to his height!

When the mind and intellect are fully developed, they grow to serve as two wings by which alone can an ego-centre fly to the peaks of the serene Light. As a mother-bird teaches its little ones to fly and play in the air, so the teacher, through these scriptural discourses trains his disciples to fly to the beyond. And in this attempt, when the mother-bird finds that the little one has landed upon the ground, tired by the maiden exertion, the mother too, perches upon some neighbouring branch.

The clamorous complaints of the little one are only answered with an equally clamorous talk from the branch! And while the noisy chattering gives us a notion that the mother is angry and the little one is in revolt, for a closer observer, it will be revealed that the looks of the little one beg the grace of the mother in love and kindness, while the beaming messages of pride and joy in the looks of the mother declare the thrilled heart of love within her. Soon, however, we find that the little one has stopped its clamour and has flown again to perch near the mother!

Similarly, in a scriptural discourse between the *Guru* and *Śiṣya*, the teacher sometimes flies to a point very much high where a sincere student cannot easily reach in one single flight; and yet, the teacher, with the instinctive love of a mother-bird, will encourage the inner personality of the student to fly up slowly and steadily to the peak where the Master stands. At rare occasions the teacher, in all love, flies back where the disciple in sheer despair has fallen down in intellectual exhaustion. At such moments, the *Guru* prescribes a dose of *Upāsanā* to revive the pilgrim to greater exertion and more vigorous endeavour.

This digression we entered in, because it is absolutely necessary for us to remember constantly the picture of the teacher and the taught behind the scripture. Thus, the *Upaniṣad-s* are highly dramatic, though therein no definite characters as such are described. Unless we remember this idea, we will not understand how and why the flow of ideas is sometimes broken, and how at rare moments, the ideas are swung into an argument that has already been mentioned earlier...which amounts to almost the sin of repetition, indeed, inexcusable in the Scriptures.

The question asked... perhaps, the question with which the student reached the Master, or perhaps, a fundamental question that must reach any man's bosom in the maturity of his own growth, is being answered here. Hence the spectacular abruptness with which the *Upaniṣad* opens.

"*In the beginning*":—Intellectually we can enquire into and try to understand the truth of a phenomenon only by asking questions like how, when, where, why, etc.; questions regarding the time, place and causation of the object of enquiry. The student has reached the Master with a poignant intellect that had tried independently to understand the world of Creation around his life. In his enquiry he must necessarily come to ask question like: "from where did all these come? What was there before the first creation? etc." The questions are being answered in the opening lines when the Master says, "*in the beginning*" before the manifested creation came into existence "*Self alone existed.*"

Entering into a cloth shop we say that before the creation of these different varieties of cloth, different in shape, colour, texture and quality, all these were nothing but cotton! Opening a box of ornaments of different shapes and patterns, of different names and valuations, of different designs and uses, we can say, before all these were created, in the beginning, it was all gold. In the same way, we are told that before the manifested world got projected, it was all *Consciousness alone..... All-pervading and Eternal.*

"*Ātman alone*":—Earlier we found in the Peace Invocation what is exactly the connotation of the terms "*Brahman*" and "*Ātman.*" Before the creation of the world *Brahman* alone remained," would have been a statement philosophically more correct; but here the Master had deliberately used the world *Ātman*. And it was not without a purpose; it indicates, indeed, the very kernel of *Vedānta*!

An enquiry into the objective world can fulfil itself only when we discover the Self in us. Cotton is the cause of all clothes and without the cotton, cloth cannot exist; gold alone is the Self of all the ornaments made of gold and the shape, design and name of the ornaments will have no existence apart from gold. Applying this truth of the world outside, the *Ṛṣi* seems to hammer this idea into the student that before the creation of the pluralistic world all that remained was the Self (*Ātman*) in the seeker, which is, of course nothing other than the All-pervading Reality, *Brahman*... for there is no difference between the cup-space and universal outer-space.

No other winking thing whatever:—Not satisfied with the positive assertion that Self alone was there one-without-a-second, All-pervading and All-full before the creation, in the same breath the *Ṛṣi* continues to point out in a negative statement that there was no other active principle or entity at that time in the Supreme. It is very well known in life that we cannot have two Emperors in the same empire at one and the same historical period. If one were to say that there were two Emperors, then it is certain that neither of them was an Emperor! An Emperor is he who has the unquestioning kingship over an entire empire. If there be another Emperor, then each Emperor would be limiting the unbounded sovereignty of the other, and therefore, neither of them could become an Emperor, true to the definition.

If before the Creation there was a Self and besides it any other active principle (as *Sāṅkhyan-s* believe that there is a principle called *Pradhāna*), then both of them would become finite in Nature. To indicate that the Self was Infinite, it was said earlier, "*all this was Ātman alone*," and in order to hammer this idea in, here it is stated that "*nothing else whatsoever living existed.*"

This idea that Self alone existed, so irrevocably expressed indicates that the Supreme did not create the world of plurality out of some material cause, just as a potmaker makes his pots from the mud, which is other than himself. In the creation of world, the Supreme itself is both the material and the efficient cause. It again points out the incontrovertible truth, which *Vedānta* is never tired to repeating that the *Creation is* but a misinterpreted vision of *super-imposition upon the Truth*, as the appearance of a *ghost* upon the *post*, available only for the experiences of the deluded and the confused.

स ईक्षत लोकान्नु सृजा इति ॥ १ ॥

Sa īkṣata lokānnu sṛjā. iti.

सः *saḥ* = He; ईक्षत *īkṣata* = thought; लोकान् *lokān* = worlds; नु *nu* = indeed; सृजा *sṛjā* = (I) create; इति *iti* = thus.

1b. He thought I shall indeed create the worlds.

Except for a couple of religions in the world which do not provide a deep and complete philosophy, all other religions, especially the six main Schools of Philosophy in India, have accepted that Creation is beginningless. This hypothesis has been accepted by all thinkers as the question itself becomes clearly unphilosophical, since we are trying to define Creation in terms of time which, in its turn, is itself a created factor.

Time, as we know, is an interval between two successive experiences. So long as we are in one experience, in the homogeneity of it, the mind cannot conceive of any concept of time; for example, when we are asleep we have no concept of time; or, while playing cards the players forget time. Therefore, time can express itself only in that mind which experiences. In order to have multiple experiences, multiple fields of objects with different relationships are necessary, since we already know that every experience must have its triple factors....(a) the subject, (b) the object and (c) the relationship between the subject and the object. Thus, time cannot be perceived and experienced unless there is a field of objects.

If we accept that the field of objects...the world... was created on a definite date and time (say, 1st of January, Friday) then there will be many inconsistencies which we cannot avoid. This day will have no existence and meaning without its previous point in time (31st December, Thursday). Thus we will have to say that a time was when creation was not started, which we all know, is ridiculous and absurd, since time itself is a created factor! All that we can say, therefore, is that the first unit of time (the second) came into existence only after the created world had manifested before our cognition. The *Ṛṣī-s* of old, instead of using a confusing statement as "the creation was started on the zero-date, zero-hour, zero-minute and zero-second," in the language of their simplicity and precision declared *the Creation to be 'beginningless' (Anādi).*

Since it is beginningless it is absurd to think of the first creation.

We have already been told by the *Ṛṣi* that Self alone existed, one-without-a-second, before the creation, and now suddenly we are told, "*he thought*;" here is an instance, wherein the scriptural brevity which pre-supposes some amount of preliminary knowledge of the fundamentals of *Vedānta*, makes a hasty reader confused to his core!

"*He thought*":—the *Vedāntik* Theory of Creation is that after the *Pralaya*, the world of beings remaining at that time in the form of *Vāsanā-s* (mental impressions) exert themselves to create a field wherein all of them could seek a complete fulfilment. And in their maturity they project forth a world that is fit for them to fully express themselves. These *Vāsanā-s* or mental impressions together in their totality, therefore, become the cause that is directly responsible for the creation of the world.

The Supreme Reality, the Infinite Consciousness, expressing through the totality of the mental impressions (*Vāsanā-s*) is called *Īśvara*, the Dispenser of the fruits of actions. This *Īśvara*—and the Infinite Supreme expressing itself as both the material and efficient cause for the world is not independent to create a world as He likes, but He is compelled to project forth a world as determined by the texture and the quality of the *Vāsanā-s* that are to see their fulfilment in the world to be created.

In a portion of the city, when we want to create a park, the contractor and his creative activity are limited by the type of people that are to come and seek their recreation therein. If children are to visit, he has to create the park with the fittings common in a children's park; if youngsters are to come to play and sweat, the contractor has to lay out fields for cricket, hockey and football, with facilities for other vigorous games, such as basketball, volleyball, tennis and badminton; if old, retired people are to use the park there are to be plenty of trees and comfortable chairs in which those superannuated men can sit around in their senile bodies and air their views ! Similarly, the Lord, the Creator...the Supreme, conditioned by the total *Vāsanā-s* in the Cosmos... is not free to create a world the better or the worse, but He has to serve the totality as a contractor would his principal!

Śrī Gopālakṛṣṇa Menon, a high official in Madras, was to retire in a couple of years time and he planned to spend his retired life in a quiet farm built on a piece of land, some three miles off Bangalore. He himself had sent a plan for his house providing one drawing-room, two bed rooms and one open *verāṇḍā* and all other conveniences. The contract was given; the house got ready, and a board "*Ānanda Vilās*" has also been nailed to the gate.

Time passed and *Śrī Memon* retired and reached Bangalore. He reached the gate of his "*Ānanda Vilās*" with his seven children and eight grand-children, two brother-in-laws and one nephew. As soon as they reached there, these eighteen members dashed into the house as any occupation army would, making an easy and complete conquest of the house. They settled themselves down—and his own dear wife, somehow pushed her way into the house and managed to be with the others. But the poor Menon found no chance of even entering in, and he settled himself down on the last step of the house sweating and fuming, complaining that the heartless contractor had deceived him thoroughly!

The contractor was summoned and *Śrī Menon* exploded himself at him. When the disappointed pensioner's tirade was over, the contractor said, "Sir, you gave me the plan: I executed the work and got the payment. As far as the relationship between a contractor and master is concerned, I have done the work and we are now quits. Of course, as a house-holder, I understand your difficulties and my heart is flowing out to you in sympathy at your unenviable predicament!!"

Similarly, we with our actions, known and unknown, conscious and unconscious, are making the blue-prints of our fortune. He (the Lord) is but a contractor who executes our plans as we give it to Him, and if we discover as *Śrī Menon* did, that we do not like the plans worked out we have to thank none but ourselves! All that we have to do is to correct our mistakes and make such extensions in our world that we re-create for ourselves the ideal world that we now demand, through right action and right living.

Though we are, to some extent, victims of our past mistakes, like the pensioner brooding over the unsatisfactory condition of his house at last did plan and execute new extensions to his house, we too can plan in the hall of this *Yajña-śālā* to make new extensions and necessary re-adjustments to our "house-of-life," so that we may find more accommodation for ourselves for a fuller existence of all the higher personality-factors in ourselves.

On the dissolution of the plurality, a bundle of *vāsanā-s* alone exist and these *vāsanā-s* exert in their maturity to express themselves, and the worlds are created.

This 'Theory of Creation' is indeed very difficult for an ordinary man to understand when he, with his untrained intellect, tries to digest the cosmic happenings. But so too are the intricate theories and arguments of higher physics, such as, Einstein's 'Theory of Relativity.' But the 'Theory of Creation,' as the 'Theory of Relativity' can be made more easily understandable if we try to perceive their applications in our own little life. Thus, objectively, if the 'Theory of Creation' is too confusing, subjectively, it becomes very easy for us to understand.

In *Māṇḍūuya-Kārikā*,[1] it has been exclusively discussed how the life in me identifying itself with the gross-body becomes the waker; identifying with the subtle-body becomes the dreamer; and the same Self identifying with the causal-body becomes the deep-sleeper. The causal-body is constituted of the deep layers of old impressions in our mind. In sleep, the gross and subtle worlds of the waking and dream merge into ourselves and while we are asleep there is, as it were, a *pralaya* (dissolution) of our worlds.

Thus when I, as a criminal and another a great saint, both lie sleeping in the same *verāṇḍā* of a *Dharma-śālā*, my world of bad intentions and his world of divine impulses both lie absorbed in ourselves. There are no manifestations of criminality through me, as there are equally no manifestations of divinity through him. But in an unmanifested condition my criminality is with me and his divinity is with him. When we both, again wake up we create our individual worlds to express our individual *vāsanā-s* so that while he finds a field to sing his songs of adoration to the Lord and inspire people to be good and noble, I find my own world scintillating with chances for perpetrating my cruel criminalities.

This state of sleep, when the individual ego is considered to be in his causal-body is equivalent to the cosmic state of *Pralaya*, when the whole world is in a state of dissolution; and yet, as in the individual, so too in the cosmic, the manifested comes to lie merged into a state of unmanifestation. That is all. Thus on waking up, I am as much a helpless victim of my criminality as my friend is irresistibly under the influence of the Divine. Thus the totality of the *Vāsanā-s* determine and order the type of world to be created. The projection of a new world takes place when irresistibly impatience and matured *vāsanā-s* press forward to express themselves.

---

1. Refer *Svāmījī's* commentary on *Māṇḍūkya Upaniṣad* with *Kārikā*.

A child cannot be kept within the womb when the pregnancy has matured to its full; in its own maturity the child quits the mother's womb and forces its way out. Similarly, the *vāsanā-s* maturing themselves push us out of the peaceful quietude of sleep into the world of activity. A typical example, perhaps, will make this more clear. Supposing you have to meet somebody or catch a train in the early hours of the dawn, say, at 4 a.m.; you find invariably that you get only a broken sleep that night and precisely you get up at just the right hour. Here, at the time of retiring, you gave a powerful suggestion to the mind and the impressions created by such a wilful planning, have been stored up which are to mature exactly at 4 a.m. Naturally by 3.30 a.m. without anybody's help the *vāsanā-s*, ready to manifest at 4 a.m., impatiently project forth and so you wake up in time for the train.

With this idea in mind, when we read the teacher's declaration it becomes clear that He—the Supreme identifying Itself with or expressing through the total *vāsanā-s* of the Cosmos desired that, "*I will create the worlds*." This is exactly the working of our individual minds when we individually wake up from our daily state of *pralaya* in sleep. As soon as we get up, ordered and conditioned by our own mental impressions, we desire for a special field or world for ourselves.

An advocate, an insurance agent, a doctor, a banker, a minister, a clerk, a priest and a cheat—if these eight people were to wake up from their sleep, the primary desires, with which they would start projecting their world should be different from each other. The advocate desires for more clients. The insurance agent wants many more rich people whom he can trade upon. The priest wants more devotees to prey upon. And the cheat demand a throng of people who have more money than brains in them!

In each of them we find that his individual desire is conditioned by the quality and the texture of his *vāsdnā-s*. In the same way, the total *vāsanā*-crowd at the time of dissolution exert in their maturity a desire to create a world wherein all the *vāsanā-s* can find a field to express themselves and thereafter creation is but a natural projection and expansion.

These fundamental ideas were very well known to the students of the *vedik* period or may be, the teacher gave exhaustive discourses at the end of which he prescribed these brief *mantrā-s* to facilitate the student to remember the entire discourse of the day. The above narrated ideas are all indicated in the statement now under discussion "*He desired to create the worlds.*"

स इमाँल्लोकानसृजत ।
अम्भो मरीचीर्मरमापोऽदोऽम्भः परेण दिवं
द्यौः प्रतिष्ठान्तरिक्षं मरीचयः
पृथिवी मरो या अधस्तात्ता आपः ।। २ ।।

Sa emāgṁllokān-asṛjata,
ambho marīcīr-maram-āpo-'do'mbhaḥ pareṇa divaṁ
dyauḥ pratiṣṭhānta-rikṣaṁ marīcayāḥ
pṛthivī maro yā adhastāttā āpaḥ.

सः *saḥ* = He; इमान् *emān* = all these; लोकान् *lokān* = worlds; असृजत *asṛjata* = created; अम्भः *ambhaḥ* = ether, space; मरीचीः *marīcīḥ* = rays; मरम् *maram* = death; आपः *āpaḥ* = water; अदः *adaḥ* = yonder, that one; अम्भः *ambhaḥ* = ether (lit. that which holds water i.e., cloud); परेण *pareṇa* = above, beyond; दिवम् *divam* = heaven; द्यौः *dyauḥ* = heaven; प्रतिष्ठा *pratiṣṭhā* = is the support; अन्तरिक्षम् *antarikṣam* = sky, in the region of (the ether); मरीचयः *marīcayaḥ* = the world below heaven, rays (of the sun); पृथिवी *pṛthivī* = earth; मरः *maraḥ* = death; या *yā* = which (is); अधस्तात् *adhastāt* = underneath; ताः *tāḥ* = that (is); आपः *āpaḥ* = water.

2. *He created all these worlds*: Ambhaḥ, Marīcī, Maram *and* Āpaḥ. *Yonder is the* Ambhaḥ, *above is the heavens; heaven is its support.* Marīcī *is the region of*

the atmosphere. The Maraḥ *is the earth and what is underneath is the* Āpaḥ.

The Supreme Consciousness working through the mass of *vāsanā-s*, in which state the world is existing at the time of *Pralaya*, becomes a personality that is capable of desiring, willing and wishing. He creates conducive worlds wherein all the *vāsanā-s* can find an efficient field to fulfil themselves. Having desired these, now in this second *mantra*, the *Ṛṣi* says that the Creator, "*created these worlds*."

Individually each one of us is doing the same in our every day life. A doctor and an advocate are sleeping in the same room and the following morning they both wake up. The doctor—meaning, the Life present in that body conditioned by his cultivated *vāsanā-s*—seeks for himself a field of patients to be visited; patients expected, operations to be performed, injections to be administered and medicines to be prescribed. Similarly, the advocate on his pillow slowly waking from his sleep behaves as a distinct personality when the Life in him acts in and through the medium of his own self-educated *vāsanā-s*, and he wishes a field distinctly different from that of the Doctor.

The advocate plans a world of his own... courts and jails, clients and clerks, other advocates and judges, affidavits and complaints, sections and cases, laws and regulations. Thus 'earning one's fees' remaining the same, the doctor's world is distinctly different from the advocate's world, since each of them desires a world in which he can play out and exhaust all his tendencies. Thereafter, we all know both of them fulfil the creation of their worlds.

Similarly, the Supreme ordered by or conditioned in or identifying with the total existing *vāsanā-s* wishes to create conducive worlds and His wish itself is sufficient: "*He created these worlds*."

When the *Ṛṣi* explained this idea to the students a surprise-formed questioning gaze—just as any one of us reading this text carefully would do—got expressed upon the anxious faces of the students: "If thus He *created the worlds* where are they? We know only of this one world, the globe on which we are living." Observing this look of confusion expressed on the faces of the students, the teacher of the scripture continues his explanation. He says the Supreme had to create four worlds so that together they become a complete field for all the types of *vāsanā-s* that are to play out and exhaust themselves in their own expressions.

In *Saṁskṛta*, the word *Loka* often gets translated into English as "the world"; this is a very poor substitute and hence our confusion in understanding the full significance. In *Saṁskṛta*, etymologically the word *Loka* means 'a field for experiencing.' The existing *vāsanā-s* 'dynamo-ised' with truth must express themselves. Therefore, these four distinct fields were created; the *Upaniṣad* gives here the names of these four worlds as '*Ambhaḥ, Marīcī, Maraḥ* and *Āpaḥ*."

These four names in themselves, again, could not convey any perceptible satisfaction to the students. For example, my friend suddenly identifies his friend and goes into an ecstasy of friendship and happiness. I watch their happy re-union and when they have parted and my friend comes to me, I will naturally ask him with all the thirst to understand who his great friend was. And supposing, he gives merely the name of the person as Mr. Chatterjee, I will not and cannot feel completely satisfied since a mere name Chatterjee does not explain the situation. Therefore, my friend will have to explain to me that they were class-mates, that they were comrades in their youthful exploits, that he had been his guest, etc. Such details distinctly give me an idea of the man.

Similarly, here the teacher said that the four worlds were created, and then, at the first unexpected enquiry, he enumerated the names of the worlds. But these names of the worlds in themselves did not explain anything to the students, and therefore, watching the confusion in their eyes, the Master of the *Upaniṣad* himself indicated the exact definition of these terms.

It is explained that the term *Ambhaḥ* means that area above the atmosphere—ether, *Marīcī*, as the term itself means in *Saṁskṛta*, 'rays,' indicates the atmospheric space. No better word can be used to indicate this medium since the rays of Sun can illuminate an object only when they fall upon it. The rays of the Sun do not either heat or light up the medium through which they pass; for example, if a beam of sunlight is entering through the windows you can see only the floor illumined; but if with a duster we vigorously dust the window or the wall, there we see clearly the beam of the sunlight slanting into the room, because all the minute dust particles that play in that atmosphere get illuminated by the sunlight. The rays of the sun falling on each minute particle illumine and thus the entire beam gets distinctly marked out against its background. The column of earth's atmosphere in which there will be always a thin suspension of dust particles in the area indicated by the term "*Marīcī*," the region of the light among the series of the created worlds.

Thirdly, there is a World *Maraḥ*, a term that signifies in *Saṁskṛt* a death, and the *Ṛṣi* explains himself in unequivocal terms that by the term *Maraḥ* he means to point out this very globe of ours, upon the surface of which mortality and finitude embrace each other and dance the tune of the song of death! The area that lies beneath the surface of the world, the region of gross *matter*, the realm of the minerals and water is indicated by the term *Āpaḥ*.

In the enumeration of these terms we find that there is a novel emphasis of sounds indicating waters; it must be because, as we all know, three quarters of the world is water and one-fourth of the area alone is covered by land.

Altogether the picture becomes very vivid if you can figuratively visualise the narration given here in the *Upaniṣad*. Imagine three concentric circles of which the innermost circle has a diameter of half an inch; the next outer one has a diameter of an inch; and the outermost has about a diameter of four inches. The innermost circle is left alone; the next outer circle is coloured all yellow; still the outer area all red, and the outermost area all blue. Then the infinite space beyond the atmosphere of this world, the ether, is represented by the blue colour; the atmosphere that envelopes the world is represented by the red band; the fertile crux round the world represented by the yellow-band stands for the stage upon which will be found finitude and death, change and impermanence, grin and roar in their heinous dance of destruction and annihilation. The innermost circle represents the world of the minerals.

These four bands—each accommodating the play of a certain type of *vāsanā-s*—in their combination become a complete and satisfactory set of worlds for all types to live fully and enjoy entirely all the *vāsanā-s*.

The statements become confusing to us only when we understand the term *loka* as world, as generally understood only a three-storeyed building wherein different types of people come to occupy its different flats and experience for themselves different layers of *Anubhava*; of course, the ground floor also serves as a store-room for the top ones!!

स ईक्षतेमे नु लोका लोकपालान्नु सृजा इति ।

Sa īkṣateme nu lokā lokapālānnu sṛjā iti.

सः *saḥ* = he; ईक्षत *īkṣata* = thought; इमे *ime* = these, here; नु *nu* = indeed; लोकाः *lokāḥ* = worlds; लोकपालान् *lokapālān* = world protectors; नु *nu* = now; सृजै *sṛjai* = (let me) create; इति *iti* = that.

3a. He reflected, "Here now are the worlds. Let me create the .world-protectors"...

Having created our own worlds, conditioned by our own desires, we generally lend our will to our plans; then alone the field actually becomes potent to play in. For example, if the advocate and doctor after planning their worlds do not throw into their plans a little bit of themselves and thus 'dynamo-ise' their desires, the fields created in their individual minds cannot by themselves provide them with any experience. We gain experiences only when our thoughts—ordered, of course, by our desires—are 'dynamo-ised' by our own sincerity, perseverance, willing and wishing, in short, by our own life-energy. Therefore, the life in us conditioned by our mental plans, which are created by our desires (*vāsanā-s*) is the "protector of the world" that we create for ourselves. This subjective world of our day-to-day creation is objectively represented in the description of the entire Cosmic creation by the *Upaniṣad*, in this *mantra*.

The Supreme conditioned by the total *vāsanā-s*—He—planned the four worlds: then He charged that thought with the Supreme Will and thus He created the protectors or rulers of the world.

सोऽद्भ्य एव पुरुषं समुद्धृत्यामूर्छयत् ॥ ३ ॥

Śo'dbhya eva puruṣaṁ sam-uddhṛtyā-mūrchayat.

सः *saḥ* = He; अद्भ्यः *adbhyaḥ* = from the waters; एव *eva* = alone; पुरुषम् *puruṣam* = the *Puruṣa*; समुद्धृत्य *samuddhṛtya* = having drawn forth; अमूर्छयत् *amūrchayat* = shaped.

3b. *Then he raised the* Puruṣa *from the waters (and) shaped it.*

After creating the worlds and providing them with a sustenance by a continuous flow of His Will-Power, in order that the specific *vāsanā-s* may find a field for their full expression, He created an instrument to express themselves and "He created a form out of water." A painter may, have artistic vision of beauty, with all details of shape, colour, proportion, setting, etc., and may also have the canvas, the colours, the brushes, and such other materials necessary; but without the instrument of a vehicle like a steady and trained hand and fingers, he cannot pour himself out in speaking colours the message of his heart on to the canvas. The worlds are created for the *vāsanā-s* to express; but the vehicle of expression, the form of a body, was needed and it was raised.

When we read thus, "right from the waters he drew forth and shaped a person," a hasty reader would get surprised, and in his ignorance may insult the *Ṛṣī-s* for their seemingly thoughtless declarations. But a careful study will reveal to us how completely scientific are the statements of these Masters. These are the days when we know a lot about dehydration process. When any living creature in the world is completely dehydrated, we know how it loses its individual shape and name, and becomes a homogeneous powder. A dead body burnt in an electric furnace reduces itself into a few handfuls of dust that it can be comfortably carried in one's pocket. All the weight and girth of dead body were, therefore, nothing but water.

Again we know that through heating, when the water of crystallisation is removed from any crystal, it of its own accord, disintegrates itself to the form of a mere powder. Thus if the *Ṛṣi* says that shape and girth were first warped out, in and from the waters, he is only expressing, in the poetic language of a heart, ablaze with the inspiration of Knowledge, the same scientific truth that is so very well-known to us today.

At this moment we must understand that the *Puruṣa* or the form created is not the form of you or me or a first man similar to an Adam, but it represents the total gross forms technically termed in *Samskṛta* as *Virāṭ*.[1] What is meant by *Virāṭ* is the rudimentary form, which anticipates the *Virāṭ*, which is yet to grow and become distinctly clear with all its features. For the time being, it is only a shape just as the shape of the chicken in the egg; the shape of the tree in the seed; the shape of a foetus in the womb, before it has taken any distinct shape at all. All the processes of development, that happen in the cosmos, are repeated by each individual in his womb. The father conditioned by his desires prepared a field and placed the seed in a medium of fluid or water, which grows in the womb into a shapeless shape, which is to develop later on into distinct organs, and ultimately gain the wondrous form of a full-grown man!!

---

1. Refer 'Discourses on *Māṇḍūkya* and *Kārikā*' by *Svāmījī*.

All along this description we, thus, see that the more we meditate upon their significances, the more are we shot up into the realms beyond the suggestions contained into these words, and from those ethereal heights gained in our meditative poise we gain altogether a new vision. We live the thrilling realisation that the totality and the outer cosmos are fully and vividly represented in each of us not only in form but in thought and experience.

"I alone am the Universe, my gross form represents the *Virāṭ*, my subtle form represents in its totality, the *Hiraṇyagarbha* and my causal body is in its macro-cosmic existence nothing other than the *Īśvara*—and transcending them all, the Spirit in me is the Supreme, the substratum for the entire world of names and forms. I alone, one-without-a second, remain revelling in myself before all these worlds were created."[1]

तमभ्यतपत्तस्याभितप्तस्य मुखं निरभिद्यत,
यथाण्डं मुखाद् वाग् वाचोऽग्निः ।

Tam-abhyatapat-tasyābhi-taptasya
mukhaṁ nirbhidyata,
yathāṇḍaṁ mukhād vāg vāco'gniḥ.

तम् *tam* = him; अभ्यतपत् *abhyatapat* = heated; तस्य *tasya* = of that; अभितप्तस्य *abhitaptasya* = of the heated (lump); मुखम् *mukham* = face; निरभिद्यत *nirbhidyata* = cleft in; यथा *yathā* = as; अण्डम् *aṇḍam* = egg; मुखाद् *mukhāt* = from the face; वाक् *vāk* = speech; वाचः *vācaḥ* = from speech; अग्निः *agniḥ* = fire.

4a. *When he had been brooding upon, there burst forth on him (the lump) a cleft in the shape of a mouth, as an egg does; from the mouth proceeded speech and from speech Fire;...*

In this section we are told how the rough lump raised from the water was brooded upon by the Supreme functioning through total bundle of *vāsanā-s*. Under the warmth of intense

1. Refer the opening *Mantra* of this section:

brooding, like an egg, the face of this shape fashioned from the waters, hatches to form a cleft in the form of a mouth. From the mouth, the capacity to express came to manifest, and from speech the cosmic element Fire rose up.

In the construction and working of the human instruments of cognition and action we not only need a physical equipment but each must have its own special capacities and each of those capacities is to be presided over by a Cosmic Power, generally called as its Presiding Deity. A modern reader need not get worried at these unfamiliar descriptions, since, when we strip the passage of its poetry, it becomes clear that what the *Ṛṣi* means here is as much scientific as the declaration of any physiological psychologist.

The physical gross "equipments" like the eyes or the mouth are, in *Saṁskṛta*, called the *Golaya...*, meaning, the organs of perception or expression. The special "sense-centre" situated in the brain corresponding to each sense-organ is called in *Saṁskṛta* the *Indriya*. Lastly, the special "capacity" to perceive, which the organs exhibit, is termed as its *Devatā,* which is, in fact, only the "material conditions necessary for each type of perception."

The instrument (*Golaya*) for the play of the power of speech is the mouth; for all of you know, where there is no mouth (*Indriya*) there cannot be any speech. The seat of activity of the mouth is called speech, and it is presided over by its capacity declared here by the *Ṛṣi* as *Fire*.

Immediately it may not be very obvious for us to realise how appropriate is the description of Fire as the presiding deity of speech. But we all know that words expressed in some speeches are 'fiery'; speeches can set an audience or a generation on fire; expressions like 'hot discussions' and 'heated arguments'—all these clearly show that Fire is the Elemental Principle behind words.

There are commentators who have explained to us that hot things consumed develop our capacity to speak; the Indian

Medical Science declares that eloquence can be improve by taking an extra quantity of clarified butter (*ghī*)! Even today in India orators and speakers—political and religious—consume, as though by their special and divine right, a larger share of the *ghī* in the community! For the hoarse throat of a speaker or a musician the treatment is to drink a glass of hot pepper-water with a spoon of *ghī* put in it. Whatever be the arguments raised by others, personally, I can endorse to you my experience that at the end of the two hours' discourse I am positively heated upto almost a degree above the normal!

नासिके निरभिद्येतां नासिकाभ्यां प्राणः प्राणाद्वायुः ।

Nāsike nirbhidyetāṁ nāsikābhyāṁ prāṇaḥ prāṇād-vāyuḥ.

नासिके *nāsike* = nostrils; निरभिद्येताम् *nirbhidyetām* = came forth; नासिकाभ्याम् *nāsikābhyām* = from the nostrils; प्राण: *prāṇaḥ* = power-of-smell; प्राणात् *prāṇāt* = from the power-of-smell; वायु: *vāyuḥ* = air.

4b. Then his nostrils came forth; and from the nostrils, the smell; and from the power-of-smell, the Air;....

The Cosmic-man that is being created by *Īśvara* (the Supreme conditioned by the total *vāsanā-s*) after gaining the organ-of-speech, next develops the nostrils. This sequence that is described in this section, I am told, closely follows the sequence pointed out by the Western medical science in the history of the development of the foetus in the womb.

First, the organs-of-smell, the nostrils (*Golaya*) burst forth and steadily the power-of-smell (the *Indriya*) developed and it was presided over by its diety the element, Air. We all know precisely that without the medium of air, smell cannot reach us as some *Attar* (scent) kept in hermetically sealed bottle cannot give us any idea of its smell, since there can be then no actual contact, between the sense-object and the sense organs, established without the medium of air. If breeze happens to be against us and we are facing the direction of the breeze, the object-of-smell existing behind us are not available for us.

Thus we can say that the nostrils can revel in enjoying the smells only when its objects are under the grace of the presiding diety, Air.

अक्षिणी निरभिद्येतामक्षिभ्यां चक्षुश्चक्षुष आदित्यः ।

Akṣiṇī nirbhidyetām-akṣibhyāṁ cakṣuś-cakṣuṣa ādityaḥ.

अक्षिणी *akṣiṇī* = eyes; निरभिद्येताम् *nirbhidyetām* = came forth; अक्षिभ्याम् *akṣibhyām* = from the eyes; चक्षुः *cakṣuḥ* = power-of-vision; चक्षुषः *cakṣuṣaḥ* = from the power-of-vision; आदित्यः *ādityaḥ* = Sun (*Devatā*).

4c. *Eyes were separated out; from the eyes, sight emerged; and from sight,* Āditya, *the Sun;...*

The shapeless lump develops into the Cosmic-man after manifesting the mouth and the nostrils and it next comes to develop its pair of eyes. The eyes burst forth (*Golaya*) and the power of vision (*Indriya*) came slowly to manifest in the eyes and it is presided over by its *Devatā*, the Sun.

This may read ridiculous to the unprepared and the uninitiated. But when we approach the description and grapple with it with necessary understanding and background, the entire meaning vividly stands out declaring its glorious message at once logical, scientific and convincing.

Even if our sight is normal and we are looking in the direction in which the object is placed, the Power-of-Vision in us does not function unless the object is blessed with light. The Power-of-Vision can function only in a medium of light; in darkness all are equally blind except some of the nocturnal animals—which are the only exceptions to the rule. Sun, we all know, is the source of all light and term *Āditya* is, in *Saṁskṛta* given to connote the light principle in the Sun.

Thus, to say that out of the Cosmic-eye, the Sun had emerged is a correct statement in the language of the *Upaniṣad*; if the Sun were not there to shed light and bless the objects of the eye, colour and form, none of us would have been able to enjoy vision and we would be perhaps, living in a dark world wondering what is the purpose of the two meaningless openings placed in the same line on either side of the nose! When the *Rṣī-s* declared that eyes are presided over by the diety *Āditya* they are but declaring this irrefutable scientific fact.

कर्णौ निरभिद्येतां कर्णाभ्यां श्रोत्रं श्रोत्राद्दिशः ।

Karnau nirbhidyetāṁ karṇābhyāṁ śrotaṁ śrotrāddiśaḥ.

कर्णौ *karnau* = ears; निरभिद्येताम् *nirbhidyetām* = burst forth; कर्णाभ्याम् *karṇābhyām* = from the ears; श्रोत्रम् *śrotam* = capacity to hear; श्रोत्रात् *śrotrāt* = from the capacity of hearing; दिशः *diśaḥ* = quarters.

4d. *Ears burst forth; from the ears proceeded hearing; from hearing, the Quarters;...*

As before in the Cosmic-man, after the eyes, developed the external organs of hearing (*Golaya*) and then came the capacity-to-hear (*Indriya*) and from it emerged its presiding diety, the Quarters.

The Quarters extending towards north, east, south and west, up and below are, as we know, all extensions of space. If space were not there, Quarters cannot exist; thus by the term Quarters they meant space.

Space is the presiding Deity of the power-of-hearing. This only means that sound which is the object of hearing cannot be created or conveyed where space is not. In order to create sound we need space; and the sound waves can travel only in a medium of air and no air can come to occupy where there is no space! Thus the space is the fundamental factor that is necessary, without which sound cannot be created. And if there be no sound then the external ear would have been as much a redundant factor as the navel pit in the human form.

त्वङ् निरभिद्यत त्वचो
लोमानि लोमभ्य ओषधिवनस्पतयो ।

Tvaṅ nirabhidyata tvaco
lomāni lomabhya oṣadhi-vanaspatayo,

त्वक् *tvak* = the skin; निरभिद्यत *nirabhidyata* = came forth; त्वच: *tvacaḥ* = from the skin; लोमानि *lomāni* = hairs; लोमभ्य: *lomabhyaḥ* = from the hairs; ओषधि: *oṣadhiḥ* = herbs; वनस्पतय: *vanaspatayaḥ* = trees.

4e. *Then the skin was separated out; from the skin proceeded hairs; and from the hairs, the 'herbs and trees';...*

Almost lastly, came the complete covering for the Cosmic physical structure in a conducive epidermis with hairy growth from its surface.

The entire Cosmic-man (*Virāṭ*) has, by now, perfected in all its details and has been clothed with the precise and definite skin which is the sense-of-touch. Hairy growth upon the surface of the total structure is beautifully put in a parallelism with the frail herbs and gigantic forest-trees on the surface of the globe. By saying so, the *Ṛṣi* indicates the entire Vegetable Kingdom in the Universe and not a special type of herbs or trees.

Just as the hairs grow on the body, not because of the individual's own accord, so too, the dumb Vegetable Kingdom without locomotion or intelligence grows from the surface of the earth. No comparison could have been so complete and perfect; the very beauty of it chokes us with a joy of satisfaction, too deep to express.

हृदयं निरभिद्यत हृदयान्मनो मनसश्चन्द्रमाः ।

hṛdayaṁ nirabhidyata
hṛdayān-mano manasaś-candramāḥ,

हृदयम् *hṛdayam* = heart; निरभिद्यत *nirabhidyata* = sprung up; हृदयात् *hṛdayāt* = from the heart; मन: *manaḥ* = mind; मनस: *manasaḥ* = from the mind; चन्द्रमा: *candramāḥ* = moon.

4f. The heart sprung up; from the heart proceeded the mind; and from the mind, the Moon;...

Continuing the same technique as before—in the same style of explanation, we are told how the instruments of thought of discrimination and willing, burst forth through the instrument, the heart. Just as the eyes were the "gross equipments" (*Golaya*) for the power-of-sight, the *Indriya*, so too, here the heart is the *Golaya*, the localised spot from which the mind, the *Indriya*, the capacity-to-feel functions. The presiding deity of the mind is the Moon.

In this spectacular expression, one is apt to get confused how the Moon can rise from the mind! But all those who know a little about the psychological behaviour of man have unanimously agreed that there is a relationship between the Moon and the mind. Lovers become extremely sentimental and emotional under the Moon, and we are not very certain whether those who discovered the phrase 'honey-moon' had not realised this relationship between man's capacity for lusty impulses and a moonlit night!

It is endorsed by all the doctors in asylums that their lunatic inmates are out of control during the full-moon. On a full-moon night any wound sustained is observed to bleed more than on other days. Thus, the relationship between the Moon and the mind is quite evident. Therefore, it is quite justified when the *Ṛṣi* says that Moon is the presiding deity of the mind.

Again in *Saṁskṛta*, Moon and mind are both called by the same term *Mati*[1] which clearly shows that in the Microcosm that which is mind, is itself in the Macrocosm, the Moon.

1. In spite of review that appeared in the "*Hindū*," when the Discourses on *Praśnopaniṣad* by *Svāmījī* was criticised as having made a mistake in saying that *Mati* is both Moon and mind, *Svāmījī* continues to repeat the same mistake for, he says, he is not a grammarian, but a *Vedāntin*. In the *Vedāntik* tradition mind and intellect are not two different entities. But they are two different aspects of the subtle body and as such *Mati* indicates as much the mind as it implies the intellect. Also when the mind is affected intellect is also affected; just as cancer in my right arm is pain and suffering to all parts of my body.

नाभिर्निरभिद्यत नाभ्या अपानोऽपानान्मृत्युः ।

Nābhir-nirabhidyata nābhyā apāno-'pānān-mṛtyuḥ.

नाभिः *nābhiḥ* = navel; निरभिद्यत *nirabhidyata* = burst forth; नाभ्या *nābhyā* = from the navel; अपानः *apānaḥ* = *apāna*; अपानात् *apānāt* = from *Apāna*; मृत्युः *mṛtyuḥ* = death.

4g. *A navel burst forth; from the navel, the* Apāna*; and from* Apāna, *the Death;...*

As before, the same sequence—the apparatus, the function and the deity—has been given regarding the vital activity of a living physical structure. In the *Hindū* Scriptures, *Prāṇa* is not Air, but *Prāṇa* means manifested vitalities of a life in a form. The expression of life in and through the physical structure of an embodied soul has been closely observed and tabulated under five distinct heads. These five departments of activity are called in our literature as *Pañca Prāṇā-s.*

Thus, the energy that functions in the sense-organs which perceives the waking-state-world outside is called the Chief *Prāṇa*; the expression of life in a living body which effectively throws out the waste matter from the body politic and also ejects out its seeds, is called the *Apāna*; digestive efficiency expressed by a living organism is called *Vyāna*; the assimilated food is equitably distributed all over the body and the vitality which is responsible for it, is called *Samāna*; and the last expression of activity in a physical body is the energy with which the mind and intellect of an individual leave the physical structure at its death and this energy is called *Udāna.*

These five different names are only the facets of the same activity called *life* in the body structure. Of them the *Apāna* is located at its headquarters in navel-area just as the power-of-vision is localised in the instruments-of-seeing called the eyes. The principle of rejection or ejection is the principle of death, and except for *Yogin-s*, in almost all the average individuals, at the time of death there is an explosive activity of the *Apāna*. It is not very difficult for any sympathetic thinker to find out the connection and come to appreciate the statement of the *Ṛṣi*, "from *Apāna*, the death."

शिश्नं निरभिद्यत शिश्नाद्रेतो रेतस आपः ॥ ४ ॥

इति प्रथमोध्याये प्रथमः खण्डः

Śiśnaṁ nirbhidyata śiśnādreto retasa āpaḥ.

iti prathamo-dhyāye prathamaḥ khaṇḍaḥ

शिश्नम् *śiśnam* = generative organ; निरभिद्यत *nirabhidyata* = burst forth; शिश्नात् *śiśnāt* = from generative organ; रेतः *retaḥ* = seed; रेतसः *retasaḥ* = from the seed; आपः *āpaḥ* = waters.

4h. The generative organ burst forth; from this organs, the seeds; and from seeds, the Waters.

In the same way as we had been so far explaining, we here also see that sex-activity is analysed under the triple heads of: instruments-of-activity, the essence-of-the-activity, and the medium in which the instrument can fulfil its essence.

Unlike the Christian faith, sex is not banned idea in *Hindūism*; the *Ṛṣī-s* don't recognise the creative urge in the biological man as the first sin, out of which the biblical world had emerged out. On the other hand in the joyous fullness of existence, the Lord's horripilation, in His ecstasy at the fullness of life lived, is the palpitating motive behind the world of multiplicity in *Hindūism*. Therefore, the *Ṛṣī-s* do not run away from the sex idea, since to suppress or ignore this activity in life is to ignore an important part in the enquiry and analysis of life as a whole.

Just as the ears are the external organs and the power-of-hearing is the internal sense-spot in the brain and the space is the 'condition' necessary for the production of the sound and for the use of the sense-organs; so too, here the generative organs, the seed-fluid (semen) and the medium or the presiding deity (water) are all indicated here.

Section ii - द्वितीय खण्ड

ता एता देवताः सृष्टा अस्मिन् महत्यर्णवे प्रापतन्
तमशनाया पिपासाभ्यामन्ववार्जत् ।
ता एनमब्रुवन्नायतनं नः प्रजानीहि ।
यस्मिन् प्रतिष्ठिता अन्नमदामेति ॥ १ ॥

Tā etā devatāḥ sṛṣṭā asmin mahatyarṇave prāpatan
tam-aśanāyā pipāsābhyām-anvavārjat,
tā enam-abruvann-āyatanaṁ naḥ prajānīhi,
yasmin pratiṣṭhitā annam-adāmeti.

ताः एताः *tāḥ etāḥ* = these; देवताः *devatāḥ* = *devatā-s*; सृष्टाः *sṛṣṭāḥ* = so created; अस्मिन् *asmin* = in this; महति *mahati* = great; अर्णवे *arṇave* = sea; प्रापतन् *prāpatan* = they fell; तम् *tam* = him; अशनाया *aśanāyā* = to hunger; पिपासाभ्याम् *pipāsābhyām* = to thirst; अन्ववार्जत् *anvavārjat* = subjected; ताः *tāḥ* = they; एनम् *enam* = to him; अब्रुवन् *abruvan* = said; आयतनम् *āyatanam* = an abode; नः *naḥ* = for us; प्रजानीहि *prajānīhi* = find out; यस्मिन् *yasmin* = wherein; प्रतिष्ठिताः *pratiṣṭhitāḥ* = being established; अन्नम् *annam* = food; अदाम *adām* = (we) may eat; इति *iti* = that.

1. *These* Devatā-s *(divinities), so created, fell head-long into the great restless sea (of change and finitude). Then He subjected them to hunger and thirst. They said to Him: "find out for us an abode wherein we may be established and may eat food (may earn our experiences)."*

So, far, the *Ṛṣi* was explaining to his disciple or disciples in the *Upaniṣad* how *Īśvara*, meaning the Supreme working through or conditioned by the total *vāsanā-s* created first of all the total gross form called the *Virāṭ,* which grew with all the external centres of perceptions, activities and internal functioning. All along the description, it was very clearly evident that the sequence in which the evolution described there is the same as the sequence in which a seed placed in the womb, develops into a foetus in the individual birth.

Poetry seems to be the very characteristic quality of the head and heart of the *Hindū.* The wondrous beauty of this land, the plenty and prosperity of our luxurious fields, the long peaceful reign that our culture provided us with as a reward for our spirit of accommodation, tolerance and sacrifice—made the *Hindū* community essentially poetic in their thought, emotion and expression. So much so, even their philosophers could not get away from the essential poetry of the age! Even the Science of Medicine was written out in poetry. We may even say that *Saṁskṛta* is no language to write in prose, the colourless commercial letters!

In this poetic exuberance, the great *Ṛṣi* explains, in this section, the various Cosmic powers that go into the constitution of a human person.

The various deities, *Agni, Vāyu, Āditya, Dik, Candra, Mṛtyu, Āpaḥ,* etc., that had been perviously described as presiding over the various localised functions of life in a human body, were created, and thereafter they were thrown into this world of endless agitations, constant changes, inner storms and outer tribulations.

Generally, the word *Devatā* is translated in English as God and therefore, the *Hindū-s* who read the English translation of the scriptures, and the foreigners who can understand, if at all, only dictionary-meaning of the *Saṁskṛta* words come to mis-judge the *Hindū* tradition of religious thoughts. But as *Śaṅkara* is never tired of indicating, the word *Deva* is used here in etymological meaning, derived from its root, which means (*Dyotanāt*) 'to illumine.' The capacity in the sense organs to illumine the world of sense-objects is meant here by the word *Devatā*.

Thus, these 'gods'—meaning, the impulses-in-the-sense-organs, to see, to hear, to smell, to touch, to taste, to speak, to die, to reproduce etc.,—all those faculties were thrown into the world of plurality constituted of the sense-objects such a forms, sounds tastes, touches, etc. Not only were they thrown into this veritable world of plurality and constant change, but they were also shot with the pains of hunger and thirst, and naturally all organs felt a thirst and hunger, at once irresistible and insufferable, to enjoy and fulfil themselves. Thus whipped up by these two impulses, they, as it were, approached the Creator and demanded separate havens wherein they can each house themselves and through the instrumentation of their respective equipments: "*we may eat food.*"

Thus, the power-of-vision demanded not an ear or a tongue, but its specific instrument, the eyes, wherein it may function and enjoy the various forms and colours, and satisfy its hunger and thirst. Similarly, all of them demanded separate conducive fields, wherein they may eke out their satisfaction through enjoyment of their respective objects.

ताभ्यो गामानयत्ता अब्रुवन्न वै नोऽयमलमिति ।
ताभ्योऽश्वमानयत्ता अब्रुवन्न वै नोऽयमलमिति ॥ २ ॥

Tābhyo gāmānayattā abruvanna vai no'yama-lamiti,
tābhyo-'śvam-ānayattā abruvanna vai no'yama-lamiti.

ताभ्यः *tābhyaḥ* = for them (gods); गाम् *gām* = (body of a) cow; आनयत् *ānayat* = was brought; ताः *taḥ* = they; अब्रुवन् *abruvan* = said; न *na* = not; वै *vai* = indeed; नः *naḥ* = for us; अयम् *ayam* = this; अलम् *alam* = is sufficient; इति *iti* = that; ताभ्यः = to them; अश्वम् *aśvam* = (the form of a) horse; आनयत् *ānayat* = was brought; ताः *taḥ* = they; अब्रुवन् *abruvan* = said; न *na* = not; वै *vai* = indeed; नः *naḥ* = for us; अयम् = this; अलम् *alam* = is sufficient; इति *iti* = that.

2. *He brought the form of a cow for them; they said, "indeed, this is not sufficient for us." He brought a horse to them: they said, "this is not sufficient for us."*

When thus, the deities created by the Lord demanded individually, accommodation and employment so that they may satisfy their hunger and thirst, Lord showed them many different types of forms where they could find the accomodation and situation to eke out their satisfaction. Thus, the Lord brought for their free selections the form of a cow, but they found that the instrument is not sufficiently elaborate to live in intelligently and experience intensively. Thus, they rejected it by saying: "*verily, this is not sufficient for us*." Thereafter the Lord showed, says the *Ṛṣi*, the form of a horse more powerful and virulent than the ordinary domesticated cow, and yet, the deities rejected it crying: "*Indeed, this is not sufficient for us*."

The lower realms of evolution are not platforms for man's higher desires to be fully satisfied; sense-objects cannot give that texture of happiness to animal, as they can give to man. In eating and sleeping, sheltering and clothing, breeding and ruling, an animal can only instinctively repeat the process, but man alone can add to these a certain amount of aesthetic values and eke out of them a joy more subtle than the mere sensuous satisfaction. Therefore, the sense faculties deified here as presiding *Devatās*, refused to be satisfied completely with the lower forms of evolution and came to demand a better and fuller edifice of man, "the roof and crown of things."

Also it is very well known in the Darwinian theory of evolution that the bipeds are evolved from quadrupeds. Thus, we must understand that by quoting the two instances, the cow and the horse, the *Ṛṣi* hints at the entire process of evolution. In all the lower specimens of forms, the sense-organs could not enjoy as completely as they wished, and the only equipment where they could ultimately find a maximum field of complete enjoyment was in the form of man; and this idea had been clearly brought out in the following *mantra*.

ताभ्यः पुरुषमानयत्ता
अब्रुवन् सुकृतं बतेति ।
पुरुषो वाव सुकृतम् ।
ता अब्रवीद्यथायतनं प्रविशतेति ॥ ३ ॥

Tābhyaḥ puruṣam-ānayattā
abruvan sukṛtaṁ bateti,
puruṣo vāva sukṛtam,
tā abravīd-yathā-yatanaṁ praviśateti.

ताभ्यः *tābhyaḥ* = to them; पुरुषम् *puruṣām* = man; आनयत् *ānayat* = brought; ताः *tāḥ* = they; अब्रुवन् *abruvan* = said; सुकृतम् *sukṛtam* = well done; बत् *bat* = indeed; इति *iti* = that; पुरुषः *puruṣaḥ* = man; वाव *vāva* = alone; सुकृतम् *sukṛtam* = masterpiece; ताः *tāḥ* = to them; अब्रवीत् *abravīt* = he said; यथायतनम् *yathāyatanam* = into the respective abode; प्रविशत् *praviśat* = enter; इति *iti* = that.

3. *When He brought the form of a man to them, they cried, "Oh! Well done—indeed, man alone is the masterpiece—Verily, man is a thing well done." He said to them "Enter into your respective abodes."*

Lastly, the Lord—the Creator, evolved most perfect physical form of the human which accommodates, apart from the sense-organs, the faculties for entertaining highly sensitive and poetic emotions, and for exhibiting an extremely powerful capacity to discriminate. The sense-organs in man, working under the sequestered shades of his wide-spread intellect with its over-hanging emotions, can milk out the maximum joy through the sense-organs. It is a very obvious truth that man is not satisfied merely because of some nutritive food but he wants it to be dressed up in a particular way and served with beauty, cleanliness and dignity; and he insists upon an atmosphere of warmth and light, cheer and melody, companionship and love in the room where he sits to consume the food.

Ordinarily, our hasty generation may not realise what I am now talking, because men and women have to hurry up to their offices at 9 a.m. when, being the slaves of their watch, they have to swallow down their half-cook food in haste, at the same time worried whether they will be able to catch their train or bus! The lunch hour also is too crowded with their office or market pre-occupations. The dinner-time is too bitter with the worries for the morrow, dis-appointments of yesterday and the sorrows of the day! And yet, what I said becomes clear when one considers one's insistence on the aesthetics on a holiday such as Christmas or *Dīpāvalī* or one's own birthday!!

Thus, when I and my dog go to visit the *Taj Mahal* or the *Mathurā* Temple, both I and my pet see the same objects. But how we react to what we see is the story of the tragedy of the dog, and the glory of its master. To the dog, it is only a shaded *verāṇḍā*, where he can run about and jump in joy and ecstasy, while to the master, it is a melancholy hall of joyous sorrow carved out in the soft polish of the stones with the sweat and labour of artisans. Supposing the master were an over-enthusiastic communist, he may find therein the wasteful excesses of a tyrant king who, with his slaves, had worked out his own personal ambition! On the other hand, a Tagore's heart sees it as 'a tear drop on the face of Eternity." Thus the sense-organs can experience a million times more subtle joys through the equipment of man and, therefore, when this form was presented to the various sense faculties, the deities cried out their appreciation and satisfaction.

A great connoisseur of music enters the 'musical mart' and tests one by one the fiddles there. During his selection he rejects many and when he gets the right note from an instrument he generally cries out—*Sukṛtam*—"*Well made, well made.*" Similarly, the faculties of perceptions and activities rejected the form of the cow and the horse, and the quadrupeds, but when they were shown the instrument of man they cried out in their satisfaction: "*well done, indeed*! *Hurrah*!!"

This is only a truth which has been recently endorsed by the declaration of Darwin that man's is the most perfect biological equipment which has not more possibilities of evolution, physically.

When the Lord, the Creator, found the sense faculties so fully satisfied with the equipment of man, He said to them you can all enter this form, and pitching your respective quarters enjoy your respective fields.

अग्निर्वाग्भूत्वा मुखं प्राविशत्
वायुः प्राणो भूत्वा नासिके प्राविशत्
आदित्यश्चक्षुर्भूत्वाक्षिणी प्राविशत्
दिशः श्रोत्रं भूत्वा कर्णौ प्राविशन्
ओषधिवनस्पतयो लोमानि भूत्वा त्वचं प्राविशन्
चन्द्रमा मनो भूत्वा हृदयं प्राविशन्
मृत्युः अपानो भूत्वा नाभिं प्राविशत्
आपो रेतो भूत्वा शिश्नं प्राविशन् ॥ ४ ॥

Agnir-vāg-bhūtvā mukhaṁ prāviśat
vāyuḥ prāṇo bhūtvā nāsike prāviśat
ādityaś-cakṣur-bhūtvākṣiṇī prāviśat
diśaḥ śrotraṁ bhūtvā karṇau prāviśan
oṣadhi-vanaspatayo lomāni bhūtvā tvacaṁ prāviśan
candramā mano bhūtvā hṛdyaṁ prāviśan
mṛtyuḥ apāno bhūtvā nābhiṁ prāviśat
āpo reto bhūtvā śiśnaṁ prāviśan.

अग्निः *agniḥ* = fire; वाक् *vāk* = speech; भूत्वा *bhūtvā* = having turned; मुखम् *mukham* = from mouth; प्राविशत् *prāviśat* = entered; वायुः *vāyuḥ* = air; प्राणः *prāṇaḥ* = scent; भूत्वा *bhūtvā* = having become; नासिके *nāsike* = from nostrils; प्राविशत् *prāviśat* = entered; आदित्यः *ādityaḥ* = sun; चक्षुः *cakṣuḥ* = power of vision; भूत्वा *bhūtvā* = having become; अक्षिणी *akṣiṇī* = from eyes; प्राविशत्

prāviśat = entered; दिश: *diśaḥ* = quarters; श्रोत्रम् *śrotram* = the hearing; भूत्वा *bhūtvā* = having become; कर्णौ *karṇau* = ears; प्राविशन् *prāviśan* = entered; ओषधि *oṣadhi* = herbs; वनस्पतय: *vanaspatayaḥ* = trees; लोमानि *lomāni* = hairs; भूत्वा *bhūtvā* = having become; त्वचम् *tvacam* = skin; प्राविशन् *prāviśan* = entered; चन्द्रमा: *candramāḥ* = moon; मन: *manaḥ* = mind; भूत्वा *bhūtvā* = having become; हृदयम् *hṛdyam* = heart; प्राविशत् *prāviśat* = entered; मृत्यु: *mṛtyuḥ* = death; अपान: *apānaḥ* = *apāna* (out-breath); भूत्वा *bhūtvā* = having become; नाभिम् *nābhim* = navel; प्राविशत् *prāviśat* = entered; आप: *āpaḥ* = waters; रेत: *retaḥ* = seed; भूत्वा *bhūtvā* = having become; शिश्नम् *śiśnam* = generative organ; प्राविशन् *prāviśan* = entered.

4. *Then Fire, having turned into speech, entered the mouth; Air having become scent, entered the nostrils; the Sun, having become the sight, entered the eyes; the Quarters, having become the hearing, entered the ears; the Deities of the herbs and the trees, having become hairs, entered the skin; the moon, having become the mind, entered the heart; the God of Death, having become the out-breath, entered the navel; the God of waters, having become the seed, entered the generative organs.*

Earlier in this chapter, we were told how the Creator raised the cosmic-man and when we were discussing the concept of the cosmic-person, we explained that it is the totality of the gross forms conceived together as one structure.

Hunger and thirst are sensations felt by an individual and they can be satisfied only by the consumption of something other than the sufferer himself. In fact, no case has ever been reported in the history of man wherein a person, because of his extreme hunger, has started eating his own fingers. Nobody can satisfy his hunger by eating himself. Thus, so long as there was the concept of the Cosmic-man in tact, the various sense-organs could not find any sense-objects other than the *Virāṭ* because the concept of *Virāṭ* is the concept of the totality. Therefore, the moment the sense-organs felt an appetite and hunger, that very moment, the very desire to enjoy something other than themselves disintegrated the *Virāṭ* concept, and, therefore, we have here the demand of the *Devatā-s* to the Creator—and the separate forms in the pluralistic world become justified. As soon as they found a fit abode for themselves they all entered into their respective organs.

In this passage we have a repetition of the same sequence of Creation explained earlier, in the reverse order. Thus, we have the description of how from the sense-organs the *Devatā-s* or the Elemental forces emerged out; while here we have the same story repeated for the purpose of emphasis and right understanding of how the elemental Forces with a deep craving to enjoy and a pernicious hope that they can have an enjoyment through the sense-objects identified themselves with the sense equipment in the individual Macro-cosmic forms.

In short, the main idea of the *Ṛṣi* is to hammer, this idea into the student's brain that the individual is nothing other than the Cosmic; from a huge piece of gold, if a tiny portion is removed, that particle removed from the main piece must have necessarily the same qualities as of gold. A basin full of pudding may be distributed in different plates, in different quantities; yet, as the pudding is a homogeneous mass of sweetness with its own distinct flavour, colour, texture, viscosity, etc., any little portion from any of the plates must have all these qualities in it.

Similarly, when out of the Cosmic-man the individuals were created as separate entities, the great *Ṛṣi* of the *Upaniṣad* with the un-said suggestions of his explanations indicates the fundamental *Vedāntik* idea that the 'Totality of the Universe'—*Virāṭ*—is intrinsically represented in the individual—*Viśva*—and individual in himself can exhibit the strength, insight and power of the entire Cosmic Form.

तमशनायापिपासे अब्रूताम्
आवाभ्यामभिप्रजानीहीति ।
ते अब्रवीदेतास्वेव वां देवतास्वाभजामि
एतासु भागिन्यौ करोमीति ।
तस्माद्यस्यै कस्यै च देवतायै हविर्गृह्यते
भागिन्यावेवास्यामशनायापिपासे भवतः ॥ ५ ॥

इति प्रथमोध्याये द्वितीयः खण्डः

Tam-aśanāyā-pipāse abrūtām
āvābhyām-abhiprajā-nīhīti,
te abravīd-etāsveva vāṁ devatāsv-ābhajāmi
etāsu bhāginau karomīti,
tasmād-yasyai kasyai ca devatāyai havir-gṛhyate
bhāginyāv-evāsyām-aśanāyā-pipāse bhavataḥ.

Iti prathamo-dhyāye dvitīyaḥ khaṇḍaḥ.

तम् *tam* = to him; अशनाया-पिपासे *aśanāyā-pipāse* = hunger and thirst; अब्रूताम् *abrūtām* = said; आवाभ्याम् *āvābhyām* = for both of us; अभिप्रजानीहि *abhiprajānīhi* = find out (the abode); इति *iti* = (having heard) that; ते *te* = to them; अब्रवीत् *abravīt* = (the Lord) said; एतासु एव *etāsu eva* = among these; देवतासु *devatāsu* = gods; आभजामि वाम् *ābhajāmi vām* = assign you both; एतासु *etāsu* = among these; भागिन्यौ *bhāginau* = share; करोमि *karomi* = (I) do; इति *iti* = that; तस्मात् *tasmāt* = therefore; यस्यै कस्यै *yasyai kasyai* = whichever; च *ca* = also; देवतायै *devatāyai* = for the god (*Devatā*); हविः *haviḥ* = oblation; गृह्यते *gṛhyate* = partake; भागिन्यौ *bhāginyau* = sharers; एव *eva* = indeed; अस्याम् *asyām* = in it (oblation); अशनाया पिपासे *aśanāyā pipāse* = hunger and thirst; भवतः *bhavataḥ* = be (you two).

5. *Hunger and thirst said to him "for both of us also find out an abode." He told them "I assign to both of you a place along with these gods and make*

you both share with them. Therefore, to whatever Devatā-s oblation is made, hunger and thirst also become partakers of it.

When thus the various faculties and activities entered the physical body at the command of the Creator, hunger and thirst not knowing where to go, remained in confusion and enquired of the Creator, says the *Ṛṣi* of the *Upaniṣad*, in his characteristic language of poetry and mysticism, "where shall we go? Give us also some abode."

The Creator found that all centres of activity have been occupied and so, instead of creating some special centre in the body for the satisfaction of hunger and thirst he said, "May you enjoy in all the centres, so that any satisfaction received through any of the sense organs would be your satisfaction."

Devoid of its poetry, if we read, the passage gives out a psychological truth. None of the faculties in man would have ever struggled to express or to develop itself unless it is goaded to do so by some dynamic impulse from within. This impluse is provided by the thirst and hunger.

We all know how a rich man's only son is invariably a poor student while a poor man's child is generally good at his studies because of his motive force to equip himself to face the competitive life. If there were no hunger and thirst for my eyes to see good things, for my ears to hear good music, for my tongue to taste good things, etc., they would be sitting down like a stone or tree in one corner striving forth to do nothing.

On the other hand, today we find women too come away, even leaving their own children, to enter the market place to fight their battles and eke out a little more earning to supplement the income of the family, so that they may have better clothing to satisfy the hunger of the skin, cinemas to satisfy the hunger of the eyes, radios to satisfy the thirst of the ears, and better food to satisfy their ever-growing thirst and hunger of the tongue.

The world today is vividly giving us the picture of what would be the chaos in the society if all the faculties in man become riddled with uncontrolled hunger and thirst that have been raised through unintelligent training to a state of "the gluttony of the organs."

Whenever any of the sense organs feel the passing flash of happiness at the acquisition of their object, for which they have been hungering and thirsting, the teacher of the *Upaniṣad* says that "hunger and thirst" will, to that extent, share the satisfaction with the sense-organs.

Section iii - तृतीय खण्ड

In this section we have a description of how food, the organic matter, was created and when so created how it ran away from the consumer's various personal functions and capacities. It was the downwards-breath alone that could grasp the food and preserve it within. It is very well-known that any given sense-object can be enjoyed only by its sense-organ, and all the other sense-capacities must necessarily fail in consuming it. For example, colour can be experienced only by the eyes; the ears cannot hear colour, the nose cannot smell colour, the tongue cannot taste colour, nor can the skin feel colour.

Later on, in this section we find a description of how the Self made Its spectacular entry into the body-form and how It had its native experience in the early days of Its entry! In short, this section forms the very core of the *Aitareya Upaniṣad*, and it stands sandwitched almost at the centre of the text-book. There are two sections earlier and this section will be followed again by two more sections; the 'peace-chanting' is common to both in the beginning and in the end.

Ordinarily this section is considered by very many critics and commentators as most confusing, and the allegories in it as most childish. In the style of the scripture, it is always the practise that simpler the style and expression and more childish the passages, the greater is the depth of their meaning and the treasure of their suggestions; the deepest ocean is calm on the surface.

स ईक्षतेमे नु लोकाश्च
लोकपालान्नुसृजा इति ॥ १ ॥

Sa īkṣateme nu lokāś-ca
lokapālāś-cānnam-ebhyaḥ sṛjā iti.

सः *saḥ* = He (the Lord); ईक्षत *īkṣata* = said; इमे नु *ime nu* = here now; लोकाः *lokāḥ* = worlds; च *ca* = and; लोकपालाः *lokapālāḥ* = guardian angels (*devatā-s*); च *ca* = and; अन्नम् *annam* = food; एभ्यः *ebhyaḥ* = for them; सृजै *sṛjai* = (let me) create; इति *iti* = that.

1. *He (the Lord) said, "Here now are the worlds and the Guardian-angels (*Devatā-s*). Let me now create food for them."*

Having created equipments of sense-organs, meaning the body, and the sense-capacities, called the *Devatā-s*, Lord, the Creator has to create the world of sense-objects for the organs to satisfy their hunger and thirst. These various sense-objects can no doubt, satisfy their individual special appetites. But the very sense-organs can themselves function only when they are fed with the nutrition that is drawn from the digested food. Therefore, the word 'food' here denotes not only the special side dishes representing form, sound, smell, taste, and touch, but it also indicates the main 'bread-plate,' meaning the nutritive food that the individual consumes by the mouth.

सोऽपोऽभ्यतपत्ताभ्योऽभितप्ताभ्यो मूर्तिरजायत ।
या वै सा मूर्तिरजायतान्नं वै तत् ॥ २ ॥

So'po-'bhyatapat-tābhyo-'bhitap-tābhyo mūrtir-ajāyata,
yā vai sā mūrtir-ajāyat-ānnaṁ vai tat.

सः *saḥ* = He, God; अपः *apaḥ* = waters (Five Great Elements in subtle form is meant here); अभ्यतपत् *abhyatapat* = brooded over; ताभ्यः *tābhyaḥ* = from the (waters); अभितप्ताभ्यः *abhitaptābhyaḥ* = from those thus brooded over; मूर्तिः *murtiḥ* = material form; अजायत *ajāyata* = sprang up; या *yā* = which; वै *vai* = indeed; सा मूर्तिः *sā mūrtiḥ* = that material form; अजायत *ajāyata* = sprang up; अन्नम् *annam* = food; वै *vai* = verily; तत् *tat* = that.

2. *He brooded over the waters, and from the waters thus brooded over, sprang up a material form. Verily, that material form, which was so produced, is indeed food.*

Just as, the Lord then brooded over the waters and produced out of it a form in the earliest creation of the Cosmic-man, so too, here, He brooded again over the waters and produced out of it the 'organic matter.' Here the term 'water' must be considered as a representative of the five elements which form the material world of substance.

It is also noteworthy here that in declaring, "*He brooded over waters and created a form and this material form is food,*" it directly gives us a definition of food. All that exist, grow and maintain themselves in water, can alone be food, and also it is a fact that food can be swallowed, retained and properly assimilated only in a medium of water. If the water element is missing, food becomes devoid of all its capacities to nourish our bodily organs. This idea is evident not only in the human and animal kingdom but even in the world of vegetable life. Seeds can start germinating only when they are soaked in water, for in a medium of water alone can the cotyledons produce the necessary enzymes which can covert the starch into assimilable food for the embryo to grow. Later on also, the tree can sustain itself only in a medium of water.

Thus, fruits, leaves and tender shoots, all become food for a vegetarian, and non-vegetarian eats meat only when it is soaked and made soft with water and cooked to taste. The declaration here clearly shows that dehydrated stuff and mere pills can never become substitutes for healthy living and if at all we consume them, they become food only when they draw the watery contents of the physical structure or the watery drinks that is supplied to the system. Nobody can live by eating the sands of the sea shore or the pebbles of the rivers or the rocks of the mountain.

Thus, it is quite appropriate to consider that food rose from the water, even in case, we are not willing to accept that the term waters here used stands for all the five elements.

तदेनत् सृष्टं पराङत्यजिघांसत्
तद्वाचाजिघृक्षत्तन्नाशक्नोद्वाचा ग्रहीतुम्
यद्धैनद्वाचाग्रहैष्यदभिव्याहृत्य
हैवान्नमत्रप्स्यत् ॥ ३ ॥

Tadenat sṛṣṭaṁ parāṅa-tyaji-ghāṁsat
tadvācā-jighṛkṣat-tan-nāśaknod-vācā grahītum,
yaddhvainad-vācā-grahaiṣyad-abhivyāhṛtya
hai-vānnam-atrapsyat.

तत् *tat* = that; एनत् *enat* = this (food); सृष्टम् *sṛṣṭam* = so created; पराङ् *parāṅ* = (the enjoyer man) turned away; अत्यजिघांसत् *atyajighāṁsat* = sought to flee away; तत् *tat* = that (man); वाचा *vācā* = by speech; अजिघृक्षत् *ajighṛkṣat* = tried to catch; तत् *tat* = that; न *na* = not; अशक्नोत् *aśaknot* = could; वाचा *vācā* = by speech; ग्रहीतुम् *grahītum* = to catch; [सः *saḥ* = he]; यत् ह *yat ha* = indeed were; ऐनत् *enat* = it (food); वाचा *vacā* = by speech; अग्रहैष्यत् *agrahaiṣyat* = (able to) seize; अभिव्याहृत्य *abhivyāhṛtya* = by merely talking; ह एव *ha eva* = verily; अन्नम् *annam* = food; अत्रप्स्यत् *atrapsyat* = be satisfied.

3. *Then the food so created, sought to flee away. He, the first embodied being, tried to catch it by speech: but it could not catch it by speech. Were he able to seize it by speech, we would have been satisfied by merely talking of food.*

तत्प्राणेनाजिघृक्षत्
तन्नाशक्नोत्प्राणेन ग्रहीतुं
स यद्धैनत्प्राणेनाग्रहैष्यदभिप्राण्य
हैवान्नमत्रप्स्यत् ॥ ४ ॥

Tat-prāṇenā-jighṛkṣat
tannā-śaknot-prāṇena grahītuṁ
sa yaddhainat-prāṇenā-grahaiṣyadabhi-prāṇya
haivānnam-atrapsyat.

तत् *tat* = that; प्राणेन *prāṇena* = by smell (by breath); अजिघृक्षत् *ājighṛkṣat* = willing to catch; तत् *tat* = that; न *na* = not; अशक्नोत् *aśaknot* = could; प्राणेन *prāṇena* = by breath; ग्रहीतुम् *grahītum* = to catch; स: *saḥ* = he; यत् *yat* = if; ह *ha* = indeed; एनत् *enat* = this (food); प्राणेन *prāṇena* = by breath (sense organs); अग्रहैष्यत् *agrahaiṣyat* = catch it; अभिप्राण्य *abhiprāṇya* = by smelling; ह एव *ha eva* = indeed merely; अन्नम् *annam* = food; अत्रप्स्यत् *atrapsyat.* = satisfied.

4. *He sought to catch it (food) by breath (smelling); He could not seize it by smelling. If he had caught it by smelling, then everyone would have been satisfied indeed by merely smelling food.*

तच्चक्षुषाजिघृक्षत्
तन्नाशक्नोच्चक्षुषा ग्रहीतुं
स यद्धैनच्चक्षुषाग्रहैष्यद् दृष्ट्वा
हैवान्नमत्रप्स्यत् ॥ ५ ॥

Tac-cukṣuṣā-jighṛkṣat
tan-nāśaknoc-cakṣuṣā grahītuṁ,
sa yaddhavainac-cakṣuṣā-grahaiṣyad-dṛṣṭvā
haivānnam-atrapsyat.

तत् *tat* = that; चक्षुषा *cukṣuṣā* = by eyes; अजिघृक्षत् *ajighṛkṣat* = wished to catch; तत् *tat* = that; न *na* = not; अशक्नोत् *aśaknot* = could; चक्षुषा *cakṣuṣā* = by eyes; ग्रहीतुम् *grahītum* = to catch; स: *saḥ* = he; यत्-ह-एनत् *yat-ha-enat* = were (he) indeed able; चक्षुषा *cakṣuṣā* = by eyes; अग्रहैष्यत् *agrahaiṣyat* = (able to) catch; दृष्ट्वा *dṛṣṭvā* = by seeing; ह एव *ha-eva* = indeed alone; अन्नम् *annam* = food; अत्रप्स्यत् *atrapsyat* = satisfied.

5. *He wished to catch it by the Eyes. He could not consume it by the eyes. Were he able to catch it by the eyes, everyone would have been indeed satisfied by merely seeing food.*

तच्छ्रोत्रेणाजिघृक्षत्
तन्नाशक्नोच्छ्रोत्रेण ग्रहीतुं
स यद्धैनच्छ्रोत्रेणाग्रहैष्यत् श्रुत्वा
हैवान्नमत्रप्स्यत् ॥ ६ ॥

Tac-chrotreṇā-jighṛkṣat
tan-nāśknoc-chrotreṇa grahītuṁ
sa yaddhainac-chrotreṇā-grahaiṣyat śrutvā
haivānnam-atrapsyat.

तत् *tat* = that; श्रोत्रेण *śrotreṇa* = by ears; अजिघृक्षत् *ajighṛkṣat* = willing to catch; तत् *tat* = that; न *na* = not; अशक्नोत् *aśaknot* = could; श्रोत्रेण *śrotreṇa* = by ears; ग्रहीतुम् *grahītum* = to catch; स: *saḥ* = he; यत् *yat* = if; ह *ha* = indeed; एनत् *enat* = this; श्रोत्रेण *śrotreṇa* = by hearing; अग्रहैष्यत् *agrahaiṣyat* = (able) to catch; श्रुत्वा *śrutvā* = by hearing; ह एव *ha eva* = indeed, alone; अन्नम् *annam* = food; अत्रप्स्यत् *atrapsyat* = satisfied.

6. *He wished to catch it by the Ears; He could not catch it by the ears. Were he able to catch it by the Ears, everyone would have been indeed satisfied by merely hearing about food.*

तत्त्वचाजिघृक्षत् तन्नाशक्नोत्त्वचा ग्रहीतुं
स यद्धैनत्त्वचाग्रहैष्यत् स्पृष्ट्वा हैवान्नमत्रप्स्यत् ॥ ७ ॥

Tat-tvacā-jighṛkṣat
tannā-śaknot-tvacā grahītuṁ
sa yaddhainat-tvacā-grahaiṣyat spṛṣṭvā
haivānnam-atrapsyat.

तत् *tat* = that (man); त्वचा *tvacā* = by skin; अजिघृक्षत् *ajighṛkṣat* = wished to catch; तत् *tat* = that (food); न *na* = not; आशक्नोत् *aśaknot* = could (do); त्वचा *tvacā* = by skin; ग्रहीतुम् *grahītum* = to catch; सः *saḥ* = he; यत् *yat* = if; ह *ha* = indeed; एनत् *enat* = this; त्वचा *tvacā* = by skin; अग्रहैष्यत् *agrahaiṣyat* = (able) to catch; स्पृष्ट्वा *spṛṣṭvā* = by touching; ह एव *ha eva* = merely; अन्नम् *annam* = food; अत्रप्स्यत् *atrapsyat* = satisfied.

7. *He wished to catch it by the skin, but could not seize it by the touch. Were he able to seize it by the skin, everyone would have been indeed satisfied by merely touching the food.*

तन्मनसाजिघृक्षत् तन्नाशक्नोन्मनसा ग्रहीतुं
स यद्धैनन्मनसाग्रहैष्यद्ध्यात्वा हैवान्नमत्रप्स्यत् ॥ ८ ॥

Tan-manasā-jighṛkṣat
tan-nāśaknon-manasā grahītuṁ
sa yaddhainan-manasā-grahaiṣyad-dhyātvā
haivānnam-atrapsyat.

तत् *tat* = that (food); मनसा *manasā* = by mind; अजिघृक्षत् *ajighṛkṣat* = wished to catch; तत् *tat* = that (food); न *na* = not; अशक्नोत् *aśaknot* = could (do); मनसा *manasā* = by mind; ग्रहीतुम् *grahītum* = to catch; सः *saḥ* = he; यत् *yat* = if, ह *ha* = indeed; एनत् *enat* = this; मनसा *manasā* = by mind; अग्रहैष्यत् *agrahaiṣyat* = (able) to catch; ध्यात्वा *dhyātvā* = by thinking; ह एव *ha eva* = merely; अन्नम् *annam* = food; अत्रप्स्यत् *atrapsyat* = satisfied.

8. *He wished to catch it by the Mind; He could not catch it by the mind. Had he caught it by the mind, everyone would have been indeed satisfied by merely thinking of food.*

तच्छिश्नेनाजिघृक्षत् तन्नाशक्नोच्छिश्नेन ग्रहीतुं
स यद्धैनच्छिश्नेनाग्रहैष्यद्विसृज्य हैवान्नमत्रप्स्यत् ॥ ९ ॥

Tac-chiśnen-ājighṛkṣat
tan-nāśaknoc-chiśnena grahītuṁ
sa yaddhainac-chiśṇenā-grahaiṣyad-visṛjya
haivānnam-atrapsyat.

तत् *tat* = that (food); शिश्नेन *śiśnena* = by generative organ; अजिघृक्षत् *ajighṛkṣat* = wished to catch; तत् *tat* = that; न *na* = not; अशक्नोत् *aśaknot* = could do; शिश्नेन *śiśnena* = by generative organ; ग्रहीतुम् *grahītum* = to catch; सः *saḥ* = he; यत् *yat* = if; ह *ha* = indeed; एनत् *enat* = this; शिश्नेन *śiśnena* = by generative organ; अग्रहैष्यत् *agrahaiṣyat* = (able) to catch; विसृज्य *visṛjya* = by emission; ह एव *ha eva* = indeed merely; अन्नम् *annam* = food; अत्रप्स्यत् *atrapsyat* = satisfied.

9. *He wished to catch it by the generative organs; He could not catch it by the generative organ. Had he caught it by generative organ, everyone would have been indeed satisfied merely by emission.*

In the above series of *mantrā-s*, we have a description of the various faculties in man that could not consume and come to enjoy food.

When food was created by the Lord, food, as it were, took flight, compelled by its instinct of self preservation, as a beast of prey would try to run away to save itself from a pursuing wild enemy. The various faculties in man, as it were, pursued the retreating food in order to seize and consume it. One by one, the various faculties and capacities in man which have been described earlier in the description of the cosmic-man have been here repeated again. Thus speech, smell, eyes, ears, skin, mind and the generative organ vainly tried to consume food and they were all doomed to failure since none of them could, in any way, gain satisfaction from the field of food.

Just as no sense-organs other than the ears can ever gain any satisfaction from sound; so too, none of these faculties could capture, consume, assimilate and enjoy food. In so elaborately repeating that none of the other faculties could enjoy or reap a benefit from food, it is only to make the student understand that each *devatā* is a limited factor and each can enjoy its special objects.

तदपानेनाजिघृक्षत् तदावयत् सैषोऽन्नस्य ग्रहो यद्वायुरन्नायुर्वा एष यद्वायुः ॥ १० ॥

Tad-apānen-ājighṛkṣat tadāvayat saiṣo-'nnasya graho yad-vāyur-annāyur-vā eṣa yad-vāyuḥ.

तत् *tat* = that (food); अपानेन *apānena* = by *apāna*; अजिघृक्षत् *ajighṛkṣat* = wished to catch; तत् *tat* = that (food); आवयत् *āvayat* = consumed it; सः *saḥ* = he, that; एषः *eṣaḥ* = this (*apāna vāyu*); अन्नस्य *annasya* = of food; ग्रहः *grahaḥ* = that which catches; यद्वायुः *yad-vāyuḥ* = that *vāyu* (*apāna*); अन्नायुः *annāyuḥ* = chief cause in supporting life by food; वै *vai* = well known; एषः *eṣaḥ* = this; यत् *yat* = what; वायुः *vāyuḥ* = *vāyu*.

10. *Then he sought to grasp it with his out-breath. He consumed it. Therefore,* Apāna *alone is that which catches food; and indeed, the* Apāna (Vāyu) *is the chief cause in supporting life by food* (Annāyu).

We have noticed that of the eight faculties and factors of perception and activity that were enumerated in the earlier part of the *Upaniṣad* while describing the emergence of the Cosmic-man, here in this section all except *Apāna* are described to have failed to grasp food and consume it. In this *mantra*, we are told the story of *Apāna's* success.

Apāna is the down out-breath, the flow of breath, the flowing movement down the alimentary canal. It is this peristaltic movement that is capable of consuming the food that is taken in and which does not allow the morsels of food swallowed down from retracing their steps and coming out. Thus the *Ṛṣi* says here, the *Apāna* is that which catches the food, assimilates, and it is due to the food so assimilated that all the sense organs are so actively and efficiently working in the body-politic in the human structure. If there be any doubt about it,, the reader is requested to experiment upon himself by a 41-day fasting, and with an ounce of water a day. When the food is thus denied to the physical body, in some 20 days, the experimenter can feel for himself, the mental, intellectual and physical abilities reducing themselves by more than half of their capabilities!

Since *apāna* grasps food, retains, consumes and assimilates it and rejects the by-products, it is *Annāyu* and therefore *apāna* is called *Vāyu*.

स ईक्षत कथं न्विदं मदृते स्यादिति
स ईक्षत कतरेण प्रपद्या इति ।
स ईक्षत यदि वाचाभिव्याहृतं
यदि प्राणेनाभिप्राणितं यदि चक्षुषा दृष्टं
यदि श्रोत्रेण श्रुतं यदि त्वचा स्पृष्टं
यदि मनसा ध्यातं यद्यपानेनाभ्यपानितं
यदि शिश्नेन विसृष्टम् अथ कोऽहमिति ॥ ११ ॥

Sa īkṣata katham nvidam madṛte syāditi
sa īkṣata katareṇa prapadyā iti,
sa īkṣata yadi vācābhi-vyāhṛtam
yadi prāṇenābhi-prāṇitam yadi cakṣuṣā dṛṣṭam
yadi śroteṇa śrutam yadi tvacā spṛṣṭam
yadi manasā dhyātam yady-apāne-nābhy-apānitam
yadi śiśnena visṛṣṭam atha ko-'hamiti.

स: *saḥ* = He (the Creator); ईक्षत *īkṣata* = thought; कथम् *katham* = how; नु *nu* = indeed; इदम् *idam* = this; मदृते (मद् + ऋते) *madṛte (mad + ṛte)* = without me; स्यात् *syāt* = can be; इति *iti* = so that; स: *saḥ* = He (the Creator); ईक्षत *īkṣata* = thought; कतरेण *katareṇa* = by which; प्रपद्यै *prapadyai* = shall I enter; इति *iti* = so; स: *saḥ* = He; ईक्षत *īkṣata* = thought; यदि *yadi* = if; वाचा = by speech; अभिव्याहृतम् *abhivyāhṛtam* = speaking be done; यदि *yadi* = if; प्राणेन *prāṇena* = by nose (*ghrāṇa indriya)*; अभिप्राणितम् *abhiprāṇitam* = smelt; यदि *yadi* = if; चक्षुषा *cakṣuṣā* = by eyes; दृष्टम् *dṛṣṭam* = seen; यदि *yadi* = if; श्रोत्रेण *śroteṇa* = by ears; श्रुतम् *śrutam* = heard; यदि *yadi* = if; त्वचा *tvacā* = by skin; स्पृष्टम् *spṛṣṭam* = touched; यदि *yadi* = if; मनसा *manasā* = by mind; ध्यातम् *dhyātam* = thought of; यदि *yadi* = if; अपानेन *apānena* = by *apāna;* अभ्यपानितम् *abhyapānitam* = eaten; यदि *yadi* = if; शिश्नेन *śiśnena* = by generative organ; विसृष्टम् *visṛṣṭam* = emitted; अथ *atha* = then; क: *kaḥ* = who; अहम् *aham* = am I; इति *iti* = that.

11. He, the Creator thought "How can all these remain without me?" So He pondered: "by which of the two ways shall I enter the organs." He again thought, "If speaking be done by speech, smelling by the nose, seeing by the eyes, hearing by the ears, touching by the skin, thinking by the mind, eating by the Apāna *(peristaltic movements), emitting by the generative organs—then who am I?*

"*Which of the two ways*" (*Katereṇa*):—The *Upaniṣad* Seer says that He, the Creator, contemplated by what door He should enter the physical structure of man, created by Him. The doubt is regarding His choice out of two different paths by which he could enter the body-citadel. In the earlier part of this *Āraṇyaka* there is a mention in the *Vedā-s* of the *Prāṇa* having entered the body by the fore-part of the feet. Self, playing the part of the vigorous activities of life, in its dynamic nature expressed in Its gross life's energy, is called

Prāṇa. In that sense the *Prāṇa* is not a different power other than the Self, but it is an expression of the same Supreme.

Though not perfect, we can, to some extent convey this idea drawing a parallel in physics: light and heat are both energies: energy expressed in the form of a cause for illumination is light, while the same energy expressed in the form of a particular impulse that gives to the skin a feeling of warmth is called heat. Both of them, we all know, are expressions of the same energy.

In the same way, for the purpose of our study, the great Master had divided the activities of life in a body into two of its aspects called the dynamic (*Kriyā śakti*) activities of physical body called the *prāṇa*, and the more subtler (*Jñāna śakti*) activity of life in the deeper layers of its implication as Knowledge or Consciousness, called the *Ātman*.

Since in the earlier part of the *Aitareya Āraṇyaka*, a mention was already made that the *Prāṇa* entered the physical structure through the foreparts of the feet, the Supreme is narrated here as hesitating or doubting as to which of the two parts should he enter!! When an occupational force victoriously marches into a capital of the vanquished power, the soldiers and commanding officers must have entered by the different minor doors of the city. But when the king ceremoniously enters the city he should not enter by the side door, through which compelled by strategy of the war, others had to enter the city. But the king will enter through the main gate.

Similarly in this body-citadel *Prāṇa* entered by the forepart of the feet and the king is to enter by a different and much more important gate. All that the Master wants the student to understand is that the grosser animal powers (*Kriyā Śakti*) in us entered by a lower gate-way, while the power of knowledge—*Jñāna Śakti*—wanted to make an entry into the physical structure by a gate which ought to be certainly a more prominent and sacred one.

If we follow the description so far made, it is evidently clear that the instruments of perception and inner activity have been first of all created. And these instruments have been provided with their respective faculties. Now in the previous *mantra*, food also has been supplied which can nourish and sustain these faculties and in their attempt to consume the food all of them get their respective fields of expression. Thus the instrument of cognition gains the capacity to cognise and the objects of cognition have all been provided so that, for all practical purposes, creation is over.

But it is like a hospital without patients, a school without students, a house without a master, a beautiful sentence without the subject. If a novel were to be written without a hero or theme it can only at best be a scrap book of description and details. If all the incidents in the text are not strung together in one chain, the novel does not become an integrated text-book providing us with a slice from the life on the day.

Similarly, the instruments are ready, efficient and strong and maintained properly; the objects are equally plenty in variety and subtle in their beauty and yet, asks the Creator unto Himself, "How can this remain without me."

The aggregate or assemblage of the various faculties, perceptions and activities, though they can individually perceive the thing and feel and function in their own fields, cannot provide for us a total integral experience. For example, let us suppose one is entering a jungle; his skin tells him that the stones are hard, that the Sun is hot; the eye tell him a four-foot long patch of green stripes on yellow background; the ears tell him the sound of a roar; the nose tells him the smell of a wild animal, and his skin tells him the touch of the sharp claws; and yet he will not be able to synchronise all these ideas together and understand at one and the same moment that the striped animal is smelling and the roar is coming from it, that it is a tiger and its embrace is not very healthy for a continued physical existence in the world, and therefore, his legs should carry him immediately to a point where the tiger will not reach.

This synchronised and unified experience which is the sum total of various reports that had reached through the eyes, ears etc., can come only when there is one Knowing Principle which knows everything through the different faculties. Without this master of the assemblage, there cannot be a purpose or fulfilment for the assembly.

Again in ancient literature in their pithy language they say that an assemblage constituted of various parts is made not for the individual parts but for a *Svāmī* (Master) who is something other than the constitutents of the Assembly. Thus a house is not built for the dignity of the pillar or the strength of the walls or the protection of the beams or the preservation of the floor. It is made, generally to house the master who is an independent entity and who can, at his will, walkout of the assemblage or walk in as he pleases. Similarly, this great assemblage of parts and faculties cannot have any justification or any sense of fulfilment without Me.

स एतमेव सीमानं विदार्यैतया द्वारा प्रापद्यत ।
सैषा विदृतिर्नाम द्वास्तदेतन्नान्दनम् ।
तस्य त्रय आवसथास्त्रयः स्वप्नाः ।
अयमावसथोऽयमावसथोऽयमावसथ इति ॥ १२ ॥

Sa etameva sīmānaṁ vidāryai-tayā dvārā prāpadyata,
saiṣā vidṛtir-nāma dvās-tad-etan-nāndanam,
tasya traya āvasathās-trayaḥ svapnāḥ,
ayam-āvasatho-'yam-āvasatho-'yam-āvasatha iti.

सः *saḥ* = He (the Creator Lord); एतम् *etam* = this; एव *eva* = alone; सीमानम् *sīmānam* = (lit. boundary of the body—*mūrdhā*) suture of the skull; विदार्य *vidārya* = having split or opened, made a hole; एतया *etayā* = by this; द्वारा *dvārā* = by that door, way;

प्रापद्यत *prāpadyata* = entered; सा एषा *sā eṣā* = that is this; विदृतिः नाम *vidṛtiḥ nāma* = named as *vidṛtiḥ* or cleft; द्वाः *dvāḥ* = door; तत् *tat* = that; एतत् *etat* = this; नान्दनम् *nāndanam* = *nāndanam* (*Nāndanam* i.e., productive of joy); तस्य *tasya* = of Him (the Lord); त्रय *traya* = three; आवसथाः *āvasathāḥ* = dwelling places; त्रयः *trayaḥ* = three; स्वप्नाः *svapnāḥ* = conditions of sleep (dream); अयम् *ayam* = this is; आवसथः *āvasathaḥ* = dwelling place; अयम् *ayam* = this is; आवसथः *āvasathaḥ* = dwelling place; अयम् *ayam* = this is; आवसथः *āvasathaḥ* = dwelling place; इति *iti* = that

12. *Then He opened the suture of the skull and entered by that door. This is the door named as the* Vidṛti *or 'cleft.' This is the place of bliss,* Nāndana. *He has three dwelling-places and three conditions of sleep (dream). This is a dwelling place. This is a dwelling place. This is a dwelling place.*

Having contemplated upon the right gateway for Himself to enter the kingdom of the body, He decided that he should enter it by the crown of the physical structure, which we all know is the most sacred and the most important of all the biological parts in us.

The soft portion representing almost an aperture or cleft, technically called by the physiologist, now, as the 'sagittal suture' is perhaps the point that has been indicated here and you all know how important is that portion which seems to be a point exposing life in us almost without any protection! This is seen in the case of new born babes very vividly where we can feel the pulse, and can, with a little pressure, feel the depression. In saying thus, that the Lord entered by this cleft or *Vidṛti*, we need only understand that the higher and the most sacred powers in man—Consciousness or awareness—entered by the crown.

The term 'entry' here is not to be constructed in its literal sense. We can enter a place where we are not already in; we cannot enter into a room in which we are now sitting. This is only a figurative explanation given of a particular sequence in an activity that was simultaneous and almost homogeneous. The *ghost* was created and then the *post* entered it, is too much of a lump of nonsense for an ordinary man to swallow down; but, perhaps, not too difficult for one who has realised or known the *post* behind the *ghost*. A pot-maker never had made a pot and then poured some space into it; in fact, he sat in space; his ball of mud remained in space; his wheel moved in space; and as the pot was made in space; its rising walls occupying or seemingly conditioning space within its volume!

Similarly, in the narration of the 'Story of Creation,' the Master was compelled to give us, in sequence, the story of the form of the body, the occupation of the sense faculties, the story of the *Prāṇa* and the manifestation of the *Jñāna Śakti*. In the description of the chemical relations or physical behaviours, in text-books of psychology—in short, in any science text-book—we find that the professors are compelled to explain to us in a narrative form, the various behaviours of the substances under different conditions, in a sequence which the student of science will have to understand as an integral process and keep this knowledge at the back of his mind throughout.

Here also your body is built in Truth, it seemingly exists in Truth, activates in Truth, gets enveloped by Truth, and pierced through and through by Truth. And yet, in the process of body's birth and growth we notice, as at the child-birth, that it is merely a shape and a primary form of a man; later on, in a few months, we find that child develops, one after another, its faculties in a sequence in which speech, we all know, is the first, and the reproductive activity the last. Thus viewed, the sequence in which the development of the

Cosmic-man which was narrated earlier seems to gather a deeper import and a purposeful meaning.[1]

It was said then that the manifestation of the faculties was in the following sequence: Speech, smell, eyes, ears, skin, hair, mind, *Apāna* (capacity to swallow down solid food) and, lastly came the generative organs and the seeds. It is only later on, in the maturity of the growth of the individual, that he exhibits the Awareness or the Consciousness in him. The *Jñāna Śakti* manifested after the expression of the *Prāṇa Śakti* in the development of the biological being, and in that sense the sequence explained here, is no blabberings of the vulgar or the ignorant, but it becomes a scientific exposition pregnant with its delicate suggestions.

The door through which Consciousness, which is bliss by nature had entered the physical structure, that cleft on the crown is called *Nandanam*,[2] meaning the place of Bliss. The lengthening of the vowel 'a' is sanctioned by a peculiarity in grammer, special to the *Vedik* Usage (*Cāndasam*). Just as we have got now India-gate, *Kaśmīrī* gate, *Ajmerī*-gate etc., similarly, this gate by which the Divine and the All Perfect had 'entered' the body is called the Gate-way-of-Bliss which alone can be precisely the right name for this mighty Arch of Entry!

If thus, the All-perfect and the Divine had actually 'entered' the physical body and if He is expressing Himself as the Principle of Consciousness or Awareness within the body structure, a doubt may come to the students as to why they are not conscious of it; and the more diligent seekers may enquire as to where they can detect at least a vivid expression of this Eternal Presence. The students attending the Master's discourses were in no sense of the term intellectual slaves of the Master. They found an honest audacity to

1. Refer Ibid. I-i-4.

2. The word used in the Verse is *Nāndanam*.... Ed.

express their doubts wherever their intellect could not follow the arguments of the *Vedik* Masters. Thus, when the teacher explained that the Infinite actually entered the physical structure, the brilliant *Āryan* students were, thought not willing to disbelieve the Seer, not at the same time ready to gulp down a vague statement however authoritative it may be.

Naturally, the great *Ṛṣi*, noticing the raised brows of the students which stood as quivering question marks on their foreheads was compelled to give a positive experimental data to prove the presence of the Spirit in the living structure.

Therefore he continues, "*He has three dwelling places and three sleeping states.*" The three states have been described by the commentators as the waking-state, the dream-state and the deep-sleep-state. In all the three states there is the play of Awareness or Consciousness.

We are *conscious of* the wakening-state-world and its experiences in the waking-state; equally are we *aware of* all the objects of the dream in our dream-condition; and lastly, in the deep-sleep-state also we are *aware of the total absence of the objects* belonging to both the other two states. Thus, Consciousness seems to play in all the different states of experiences and the awareness commonly exhibited in all the three states—Awareness as such—is defined here as or demonstrated as the *Ātman* or the Reality which had entered the physical structure.

Not only has the *Ātman*, as it were, Its three different manifestations as the waker, as the dreamer, and as the deep-sleeper[1], but in each condition the Self in us seems to monopolise for itself a localised abode in our structure. The reader should not take these statements too literally. These are statements made during the narration of the Creation-story, which the Seer started with a declaration of the unadulterated

---

1. For more details refer Discourses on *Māṇḍūkya* and *Kārikā*" by *Svāmī Chinmayāṇanda*, wherein these three states have been exhaustively dealt with.

Truth in the very opening *mantra* of the *Upaniṣad*; "*In the beginning before Creation, Ātman alone existed....one-without-a-second.*"

Thereafter the details of the Creation have been described as a development in the technique of *Āropa* and *Apavāda*[1]. To make the story complete and give its empty sketches the flush of throbbing life, here the Master goes to the extent of saying that the Supreme arrogates to Itself some camp-headquarters in the three planes of Its experiences! These three camp-quarters are indicated by the teacher during his discourses to the student, "with a didactic gesture"—meaning, the teacher must have pointed out with his index finger the three parts on his own physical structure.

The idea of an extra concentration of our individual ego-centric awareness in different places in ourselves during the different states of experiences was, perhaps, at that time the knowledge of the plough-man and the pot-maker, the weaver and the householder, so that the Master had not to explain the implication, but had only to point out those centres in the physical structure. According to *Śaṅkara* the camp-head-quarters of the Self in the waking-state is in the right eye, in the dream-state it is in the throat, and in the deep-sleep-state it is in the heart-space.

To a large extent you and I can experimentally feel for ourselves that there is an extra quantity of ego-centric arrogation for us, in our waking-state, at the point represented by the right-eye. Supposing in a crime committed by me the judge declares that I can choose between my leg or my hand that must be cut off; I will certainly offer my hand, if my dismemberment is unavoidable! If the choice is between the right and the left hands, I will offer the left, because the right seems to be the more sacred and useful. If the choice is between the nose and the eyes, I will rather offer my nose

1. For details refer to Page 15 in the 'Introduction Section.'

and not the pair of eyes. Of the two eyes, I will certainly offer the left-eye and not the right-eye.

Thus, if you sit down quietly and decide the things which you will be prepared to sacrifice and the relatively more sacred spots you will preserve to the last, the thing that you will like to possess till the end will be invariably the right-eye. This you will like to keep on as the last citadel to fight for and defend, except of course, in case of persons suffering from cataract in the right-eye. Thus, there seems to be an extra concentration of the waking-stage-ego in the right-eye. So too, in the dream-state, the *Yogaśāstra* claims that there is at the throat a kind of over centralisation of the dream-ego, and it also points out that in the deep-sleep-state individualistic personality folds up its various impressions and comes to dwell in the heart-space.

In short, we must note carefully that the teacher is trying to answer the unasked question of the disciple as to where exactly is this Conscious Principle revelling in us, if it had entered the structure, as the scriptures had explained. Consciousness functions in the three states of man's experiences and in all the *avasthā-s,* we are conscious of the objects belonging to each state. Herein, through an indirect method, the existence of the Consciousness has been described as That which makes it possible for the individual to bring the objects of the waking, dream and deep-sleep-state, within the purview of his Awareness. That, which makes things available for our perception and understanding, is Consciousness.

These states as well as the various dwelling places are all very clearly explained here as belonging to it (*Tasya).* When we say *Rāma's* buffalo,' we mean that buffalo which belongs to *Rāma*; it does not mean that *Rāma* is himself a buffalo. Whenever we use possessive nouns the things possessed belong to the possessor, and the possessor is distinctly different from the thing possessed. The *Ṛṣi* by saying here that the states and the places of dwelling belong to the

Consciousness, he means that Consciousness is the possessor, the owner, the Lord, of the three states and the owner of the dwelling places. The waking, dream, and deep-sleep states are not in themselves Consciousness; It plays in the three fields and gives to them their meaning and substance.

स जातो भूतान्यभिव्यैख्यत्
किमिहान्यं वावदिषदिति ।
स एतमेव पुरुषं ब्रह्म
ततममपश्यत् । इदमदर्शमिती३ ॥ १३ ॥

Sa jāto bhūtany-abhivyaikhyat
kimi-hānyaṁ vāva-diṣaditi,
sa-etam-eva puruṣaṁ brahma
tata-mam-apasyat, idam-adarśam-itī 3.*

सः *saḥ* = he; जातः *jātaḥ* = having born; भूतानि *bhūtani* = beings, creatures; अभिव्यैख्यत् *abhivyaikhyat* = gazed around; किम् *kim* = who, what; इह *iha* = here; अन्यम् *anyam* = other; वावदिषत् *vāvadiṣat* = can I proclaim or name; इति *iti* = thus; सः *saḥ* = he; एतम् *etam* = this; एव *eva* = verily; पुरुषम् *puruṣam* = *Puruṣa*; ब्रह्म *brahma* = the *Brahman*; ततमम्** *tatamam* = over spreading all; अपश्यत् *apasyat* = realised, saw; इदम् *idam* = this (*Parabrahma Paramātmā*); अदर्शम् *adarśam* = (I have) seen; इति *iti* = that.

13. Having been born, he looked around on beings. He gazed around upon the creatures. How should he speak of any other? "What else is there besides

---

* In *Vedik* texts, the figure '3' appearing after the word '*iti*' indicates prolongation of sound in '*i*' in accordance with the rule that in case of a word suggesting liberation, the vowel gets lengthened. ...... Ed.

** *Śaṅkara* reads it as *tata-tamam* (by adding the missing *ta*) to mean the most pervasive, the fullest, like space...... Ed.

the Ātman *for Me to name?" He saw verily this very* Puruṣa, *the* Brahman, *over-spreading all. With wonder he said to Himself "Oh, I have seen this."*

The language in this *mantra*, if literally translated will disclose that it is extremely broken with a dozen emotional pauses ... and it is, as it should be, at all dramatic moments. When emotion overpowers thought and when ideas get fired up to its white-heat of intensity, language does not conform to the conventional rules of grammer and syntax, but, as it were, evaporates here and there into explosive amazement or wonderment!!

At the impact of the breathless ecstasy in which one realises the Self, when It is described, naturallly, the language should be as it is here—broken, stammering, halting. In the above rendering we have not cared to translate the *mantra* literally, but have paraphrased the passage lending to it all its missing links and we have taken freely the liberty to fill in the gaps as best as we can.

On the whole the passage tries to describe the experience of Self when It—having entered the physical body in its native purity, wisdom and Self-knowledge—looked out upon the pluralistic phenomenal world through the various equipments of the sense-organs, the mind and intellect, when It could, in and through the sense-objects, emotions and ideas, perceive nothing but Its own essential nature everywhere!! At the perception of this *Puruṣa* over-spreading all, He cried out, in the ecstasy born out of the Divine inspiration which is the lot of everyone experiencing that tranquillity of a stilled mind, "Oh! I have seen *this*."

The *Ātman* or the Self is indicated in the *Vedāntik* literature by the pronoun "*this*." Without a little acquaintance with the covenants of *Vedānta*, it is very difficult for the student to come to appreciate the depth of significance by the pronoun "*this*."

We all know that we use the pronouns "*that*" and '*this*' to indicate two things, the former relatively farther from us than the latter: the nearer one is always indicated by the pronoun '*this.*' Thus as an example: regarding a series of things that lie between the things nearest to us and that distant wall, we will be always using the term '*that*' to indicate the object which is farther from us and the term '*this*' to the object relatively nearer to us. Thus *that wall* and *this table*; *that table* and *this book* in my hand; that book and *this shirt* on me; *that shirt* and *this mind*; and *that mind* and *this intellect...* and so on, we will be *always indicating the nearer object with a pronoun 'this.'*

A time then should come, therefore, when we shall reach a point in us which will be, as it were, an '*Absolute this,*' which in its turn cannot be ever indicated by a pronoun '*that*' with reference to anything nearer to us. That subjective centre— which is nearest to us, so near that there is no other point with reference to which, It can ever be a '*that*' is best defined as '*this.*'

With this knowledge of the sacred meaning, and the tradition of the usage of the word '*this*' in *Vedānta*, we shall get easily introduced into the vast amphitheater of beauty that lies so secretly concealed in this passage. "*Oh, I have seen this.*"

The passage, as such, only means that the Self—"*the Self alone was before Creation*"[1]—having created the form and having housed the various faculties of vision, etc., in it, when He consciously entered without any self-forgetfulness, and gazed out into the world of plurality through the equipments of vision and knowledge, could yet realise and experience His own transcendent nature and enjoy His own divinity reflected in and through the pluralistic world.

---

1 Refer Commentary on I-i-1 (Pages 27 to 39).

The endless suggestion of serenity and wisdom, hope and glory, that should thrill any student of the scripture when he meditates upon the implications of the passage, is almost inexhaustible. Everyone of us is a proto-type of the First Person that was separately created and into whom the Supreme entered, and, therefore, if we can even now, detaching ourselves from all our false identifications with the body, mind and intellect, in our own Divine Nature as Consciousness, look out into the world outside, we shall still detect that Truth which is the substratum, permanent, unchangeable, tranquil, all-perfect, immortal and blissful revelling everywhere! At the experience of this, every one of us shall cry the same song of wondrous ecstasy, "*Oh, I have seen this.*"

The word "seen" used here does not imply the method of vision which we experience in our ordinary walk of life. Ordinarily, we see things that are separate from ourselves, at the interplay of the instrument-of-vision, wherein the seeker is different from the thing seen and the experience of seeing is accomplished when a definite relationship is set up between the subject and the object.

But in Self-realisation (*Ātma Sākṣātkāra*) it is only the Self, seeing the Self, and here the word 'seen' is used in a special connotation. To see an object is to believe it, is to understand and to know it, without even an iota of doubt regarding its reality for the Seer. By saying that the Self is seen, the *Vedāntin* only means that the experience of the Self, shall be so conclusive, and so fully beyond all doubts and conclusions that it shall be as convincing *as though one has seen the Self.*

तस्मादिदन्द्रो नामेदन्द्रो ह वै नाम ।
तमिदन्द्रं सन्तमिन्द्र इत्याचक्षते परोक्षेण ।
परोक्षप्रिया इव हि देवाः
परोक्षप्रिया इव हि देवाः ॥ १४ ॥

Tasmād-idandro nāmedandro ha vai nāma,
tam-idandraṁ santam-indra ityā-cakṣate parokṣeṇa,
parokṣa-priyā iva hi devāḥ,
parokṣa-priyā iva hi devāḥ.

तस्मात् *tasmāt* = therefore; इदन्द्रः नाम *idandraḥ nāma* (इदम् *idam* is this and द्र *dra* is seeing) = named or called *Indandra*; इदन्द्रः ह वै नाम *idandraḥ ha vai nāma* = verily known as *Idandraḥ;* तम् इदन्द्रम् सन्तम् *tam idandram santam* = Him who is *Idandra;* इन्द्रः इति *indra iti* = as *Indra*; आचक्षते *ācakṣate* = is called; परोक्षेण *parokṣeṇa* = indirectly; परोक्षप्रिया: *parokṣa-priyā* = fond of the cryptic (indirect names); इव *iva* = verily; हि *hi* = is it; देवा: *devāḥ* = *Devā-s*; परोक्षप्रिया: *parokṣa-priyāḥ* = fond of cryptic (indirect names); इव *iva* = verily; हि *hi* = as it were; देवा: *devāḥ* = *Devā-s.*

14. *Therefore, He is called* Idan-dra *(*Idam......*it; dra.....seeing: 'It-seeing').* Idandram, *verily, is His name. Though he is* Idandra, *He is indirectly called as* Indra, for Devā-s *are fond of the cryptic (indirect names); the gods are indeed fond of being called, as it were, by indirect names.*

Because he saw the All Pervading *Brahman*, subjectively as '*this*' (*Idam*) the Supreme Truth is called as *Idandra*. Since gods are fond of being called by their mystic names He is called *Indra.* *

In our life also when we have to show respect and reverence to some people, we do not address them by their personal names but would address with their titles as the Prime Minister, Your Honour, Your Lordship, Your Majesty, Inspector *Sāheb*, *Bābujī*, etc. Apart from these, a thousand

---

* *Śrī Śaṅkara* points out that Gods love mystery and are fond of being referred to indirectly, that is, to be behind the veil, because they are worthy of great adoration. We find this idea also in *Bṛhadāraṇyaka Up.* (IV-ii-2); *Śatapatha* (VI-1-1-2 and VII-5-1-22) and also in *Aitareya Brāhmaṇa* (III-43-1). ...Ed.

other examples can be taken from our home life where we do not call our mother as "our father's wife," nor does in India, except in rare perverted cases, the wife indicates her husband directly by his name.

Where we feel respect and reverence there we do not generally address the individual directly by his personal name, but we use generally either a pet name or reverential appellation for a revered man, good and noble, a man who is a noted genius in his own walk of life. "*Devāḥ*" is essentially one who appreciates when addressed* indirectly—*Parokṣa-priyāḥ*. Though, *Idandra* should verily be His name, He is thus, out of respect, called by a shorter appellation *Indra*.

CHAPTER II

Section i - प्रथम खण्ड

(अपक्रामन्तु गर्भिण्यः)

पुरुषे ह वा अयमादितो गर्भो भवति ।
यदेतद्रेतः तदेतत् सर्वेभ्योऽङ्गेभ्यस्तेजः
सम्भूतमात्मन्येवात्मानं बिभर्ति ।
तद्यदा स्त्रियां सिञ्चत्यथैनज्जनयति
तदस्य प्रथमं जन्म ॥ १ ॥

(Apakrāmantu garbhiṇyaḥ)

Puruṣe ha vā ayamādito garbho bhavati,
yadetad-retaḥ tadetat-sarvebhyo-'ṅgebhyas-tejaḥ
sambhūtam-ātmanyev-ātmānaṁ bibharti,
tadyadā striyāṁ siñcatya-thainaj-janayati
tadasya prathamaṁ janma.

(अपक्रामन्तु गर्भिण्यः) *(Apakrāmantu garbhiṇyaḥ)* = (the pregnant women may please vacate).

पुरुषे *puruṣe* = in the man; ह वै *ha vai* = verily; अयम् *ayam* = this; आदितः *āditaḥ* = at first; गर्भः *garbhaḥ* = embryo; भवति *bhavati* = becomes; यत् *yat* = which; एतत् *etat* = this is; रेतः *retaḥ* = seed; तत् *tat* = that; एतत् *etat* = this; सर्वेभ्यः *sarvebhyaḥ* = from all; अङ्गेभ्यः *aṅgebhyaḥ* = from parts; तेजः *tejaḥ* = strength (and vigour); सम्भूतम् *sambhūtam* = is accomplished (extracted) as essence, vigour; आत्मनि *ātmani* = in the Self; एव *eva* = indeed; आत्मानम् *ātmānam* = the Self; बिभर्ति *bibharti* = bears; तत् *tat* = that; यदा *yadā* = when; स्त्रियाम् *striyām* = into a womb; सिञ्चति *siñcati* = pours; अथ *atha* = then; एनत् *enat* = this; जनयति *janayati* = makes it born; तत् *tat* = that is; अस्य *asya* = his; प्रथमम् *prathamam* = first; जन्म *janma* = birth.

[*The pregnant women may please vacate*]

1. *In a man, verily, this one becomes at first that germ which is called the seed. That which is semen is the essence of strength and vigour, drawn from all his limbs. In the Self, indeed, one bears the Self. When he pours this into a womb, he causes it to be born. This is its first birth.*

In this section, we have a detailed description of the various stages through which the metamorphosis takes place before a father becomes himself his own son! *Vedānta* not only explains the oneness of the Universe but also describes a rigid scheme of arguments and observations by which it is rendered easily possible for us to realise the exact connection that makes one intimately connected with the others.

Here in this chapter the process of procreation is analysed, and viewed from the standpoint of philosophy wherein the science of sex becomes only hand-maiden. Biologically we know how the seed deposited in the womb grows itself to be the foetus, which, it its maturity emerges out as a child. But here the same process is viewed from a delicately divine and subtly philosophical standpoint, and with as many strokes as possible, the *Ṛṣi* has tried to indicate the entire picture of the essential oneness of the father with the son. If this is once realised, the unit of a society, which, indeed, is the home, will be properly reorganised and when the home is organised well, the community, society, nation, even the world will organise themselves upon a much more equitable sense of mutual understanding and with a deeper sense of mutual love and brotherhood.

In the very opening of the section there is, as it were, a dramatic direction in which the *Guru* is requesting the pregnant women in the assembly to retire for some time; and at the end of the section, we shall find that he again requests them to re-enter the hall of study. This instruction would have become redundant and meaningless if women were not students of *vedāntik* discourses given by the teachers. This passage forms an integral part of the *Vedā-s* and, therefore, should be taken as a definite internal proof to show that *Hindū* women used to have, in those days, free access to the great teachers and ready admission into their discourses.

It was only later on that *Hindūism* started decaying and, in the days of its decay, a self-seeking priest-class had deliberately molested the glowing purity and healthy vigour of our tradition. What exactly were the historical forces that perverted a wise group of men to behave against their own culture are not very clear at present, for a student of our history. Whatever be the cause, or the causes, we find that somewhere along the avenue of time the children of the *Āryan* stock missed their way and brought themselves and their great-grand-children, who were blindly following their immediate predecessors, into a sad plight in which we find ourselves today.

This 'stage direction' now under discussion paints for us the entire picture of the *Āśrama*. There, the great *Ṛṣi* instructed and initiated his chosen disciples into the great sacred knowledge of *Vedānta*, and the class-rooms were wide open for others who were interested in knowing their religion; all were encouraged to come and listen without disturbing the class. The tradition followed in the *Himālayā-s* even today must be a distant echo of what they practised then. My *guru*[1]

---

1. *Svāmī Chinmayānanda* was initiated into *Vedānta* by H.H. *Śrī Svāmī Tapovanajī Mahārāja* of *Uttarakāśī*....Ed.

for instance, did not allow everybody to attend the classes of the *Upaniṣad* studies, "with a text-book in their hands," when he was teaching me. But at the same time many *mahātmā-s* and house-holders used to come to the same *varāṇḍā* of the *Tapovana Kuṭīra* and regularly attend *Śrī Gurudeva's* discourses. But none of them was allowed to keep a book in hand and learn at the Master's feet—unless, of course, he had been accepted earlier by the teacher, as a student for the studies.

Similarly, in the ancient days too, while the great *Ṛṣi* initiated their disciples into *Vedānta*, men of all stages of life, of all temperaments, titles, status, and even women of all ages and under all conditions such as pregnancy etc., were regular visitors who faithfully attended the daily-lectures.

On the opening of this section, all women are not requested to go; only those who are in the 'family way' are asked to retire for a short duration during these five *mantrā-s* not because of any want of sympathy for time, but it was in dutiful obedience to a great psychological truth. Psychology was seemingly so very well developed in the days of the *Vedā-s* that the teachers had made use of their knowledge of the human mind at every moment in all their contacts with their disciples in particular and the society in general.

At the first reading of this 'stage direction' without this general knowledge, one is apt to believe that the teachers were against women listening to the *Vedāntik* discourses or certain portions of the *Vedā-s*. This misunderstanding comes not only from the foreigners, but also, even the orthodox *paṇḍita-s* in their hasty conclusions and blind estimates of the *Hindū* tradition practised their fallacious theories and brought about or at least hastened the calamitous fall of *Hindūism*.

The *Pūrāṇā-s* gave a hundred different instances which clearly provide us with conclusive evidence that the Masters fully understood the individual and the communal psychology of the *Hindū-s*, and the *Ṛṣī-s* consistently put into practise the knowledge of their psychology for preparing a healthier social life, and also in avoiding all strains and stresses upon the mental personalities of the seekers during their spiritual pilgrimage to Truth.

In the *Purāṇā-s* there is a very interesting portion where we are told how *Indra* got very anxious on realising that the demon *Hiraṇyakaśipu's* had reared a generation of secularism devoid of any sense of sacredness, and had raised almost a generation of *Hiraṇyakaśipū-s*. At this time the emperor took a holiday and retired to the jungles to perform more *tapas* and acquire for himself greater mental strength and intellectual poise to accomplish his thoughtless schemes of devastating the Immortal *Hindū* culture. *Indra*, in order to avert this calamity, ordered that every pregnant woman in that kingdom must be segregated immediately until her confinement, after which, the mother could be sent back home so that the rising generation be saved from a calamitous degeneration.

We are told in the story that *Nārada* who was coming at that time met *Indra* personally conducting the great consort of *Hiraṇyakaśipu*, who was then herself pregnant. On seeing them *Nārada* enquired and when the great sage heard the intentions of *Indra*, *Nārada* requested the King of Gods to let him have his method of cure administered to the noble lady.

Indra surrendered her to him and the kindly Sage of Wisdom and Devotion conducted her to *Vasiṣṭha's āśrama*, where she remained till the fullness of her pregnancy, in the serene atmosphere, listening to the daily discourses and serving the *Āśrama* in her own devoted way. The queen was sent back at the proper time to her palace. The Emperor returned; the boy of the *Purāṇā-s*, the devoted *Prahlāda* was born.

The story clearly reveals the working of a modern psychological theory that in the nurseries and schools, in the colleges and public life, men can be slowly converted into better or worse types. But pre-natal education is a method or theory that is of the most recent origin in the west, and they claim for themselves the credit of having discovered it, as if they were the first discoverers of this idea. But when we turn to the ancient literature of the *Hindū-s,* we find that this theory or knowledge had been in this country almost from the *Vedik* period when they exhaustively made use of the idea in their planning of the society for its cultural growth and eminence.

If the food which the mother takes, in its assimilated form goes into the production of the body and form of the child in her womb, then to a great extent the thoughts of the mother during her pregnancy give a direction and an impetus to psychological make-up of the child. Innumerable cases have been discovered and reported wherein the child, born of a mother who had a severe shock of or fright during her pregnancy, had developed hysteria, nervous debility, epilepsy, etc. And the modern mother who revels with voluptuous films and spends her evenings in revelry and excesses, and lives a life of ignoble lust, consciously moulds the character of the child in such a way that even before puberty the children of such mothers cause a national problem in general immorality.

Since this section explains the various stages in which the child grows from the moment of the insemination, the *Ṛṣi* felt that, perhaps, the pregnant mothers would thereby come to entertain sex thoughts which, in their turn, might harm and destroy the mental life of a child of *Hindūism* that is yet to be born! Hence the instruction, "*Pregnant women, please retire.*"

The passage now under discussion vividly brings to our vision the entire mournful pilgrimage of an ego-centric impulse, which patiently throbbed to enter into a greater self-manifestation—viz., from the stone-life, the vegetable and the animal kingdoms, progressively to the luxury of a chance to be a human by birth. Manifested at first as an indeterminate thin point in stone-life, the *Jīva* (ego-centre—yet unmanifest) had to wait for an indefinitely long time, until at last a causal sweep of Nature's slow hammers, in the form of rain and heat, crumbles the stone into minute particles. As particle, it might have waited for millions of years before a chance root passing by embraced it to suck in.

It may then become a leaf or a bark, portion of the trunk or a wee-bit of some stock or petal, and going back again up the ladder. Supposing it becomes a fruit on the tree: the chances are, one to hundred, that it may fall down, and again become one with the earth. An animal having eaten the fruit may produce out of it a part of its bone, and we know how long it will have to wait until at last it can afford to become again a morsel in the mouth of animal! Supposing, it again becomes a fruit and is eaten by an animal which is the prey of yet another animal!

In this vicissitude of chances flowing pell-mell, it is indeed a rare chance that the fruit is eaten by a cow and that the fruit becomes its milk: it *again* some-how or other escapes the calf-mouth and becomes the milk collected, and *again*, that milk is not drunk by the domesticated cat, but actually goes into the mouth of the father, where, *again*, it may become a part of his bone!

Supposing, again, the lucky *Jīva* now present in the cup of milk drunk by the father actually happens to become a seed in him, and among the thousands of seeds wasted, this luckiest of them again happens to enter the womb of a sensible mother, healthy and good so that it, after all, in the end, gains the form of human structure—healthy and hearty with an equally healthy and efficient mind and intellect, like most of us here in the *Yajñaśāla*! How rare, indeed, is the chance for a human birth, and yet, how rarely if at all, do we, nowadays, realise the sacredness of life and employ it intelligently for the higher purposes of living a nobler life.

No doubt the above is an exaggerated version of the story of evolution as seen through the gogles of the philosopher. But it brings vividly to our mind's eye the sacredness of the human birth, and, therefore, the heavier is the responsibility that rests with us in making our life a successful mission and reach altogether greater perception in this very life.

In the *mantra*, it is said "*this one becomes at first the germ.*" Here '*this one*' (*Ayam*) means the Supreme conditioned by the individual's *vāsanā-s* moving about with a mind-and-intellect which is the product of its entire past life in thought and action. This entity is called the *Jīva*. It is moving about demanding and expecting a fit vehicle through which to gain for itself a complete fulfilment of all its desires in the world of experiences. This entity has been already explained in the previous portions of the text, and *this one* first of all manifestes itself as potent sperm in an individual.

That the reproductory fluid is the essence of the assimilated food is not a modern biological discovery, but it is an old information that was available even in the *Vedik* period is very well indicated here when the *mantra* says that the seminal fluid is the "*essence of strength and vigour drawn from all his limbs.*"

Therefore, every seed in man is the essence of that individual and as such philosophically we may say that one lives as the seed in one-self. In this sense the *mantra* but declares an obvious philosophical truth when it says "*In the self, indeed, one bears the Self.*"

The seed is nothing but a miniature of oneself. When it is poured into the reproductory system there is an emergence of the man out of himself. In this sense we may say that the first birth of that individual being is when, as a seed, it emerges out or it is delivered into the womb.

Ordinarily, we call it a birth when the child is thrown out from the womb into a field, where it can find a favourable atmosphere to continue its growth and expression, in the outer world. When individual in the form of a seed is placed in the womb, it being the right world where the sperm can find a conducive atmosphere to grow into a more developed expressiveness, this is considered as a birth in itself.

Thus, philosophically, we may say that he is born again when an individual throws his seed in the womb of his partner. The physiologist may read in this a pleasant contradiction; philosophically it is only too true to say so.

तत्स्त्रिया आत्मभूतं गच्छति ।
यथा स्वमङ्गं तथा ।
तस्मादेनां न हिनस्ति
सा॒स्यैतमात्मानमत्रगतं भावयति ॥ २ ॥

Tat-striyā ātma-bhūtaṁ gacchati
yathā svamaṅgaṁ tathā,
tasmād-enāṁ na hinasti
sāsyaitam-ātmānam-atragataṁ bhāvayati.

तत् *tat* = that (seed); स्त्रिया *striyā* = with the woman; आत्मभूतम् *ātmabhūtam* = of (her) own; गच्छति *gacchati* = becomes; यथा *yathā* = as; स्वम् *svam* = one's; अङ्गम् *aṅgam* = limb; तथा *tathā* = like that; तस्मात् *tasmāt* = therefore; एनाम् *enām* = to this (woman i.e. mother); न *na* = not; हिनस्ति *hinasti* = hurt, injure; सा *sā* = she (that woman); अस्य *asya* = his (her husband); एतम् *etam* = this (seed); आत्मानम् *ātmānam* = Self; अत्रगतम् *atragatam* = thus (having) come to her (body); भावयति *bhāvayati* = nourishes.

2. *That seed becomes one with the woman, just as a limb of her own. Therefore, (the foetus) does not injure her. She nourishes this Self (of her husband), that has thus come to her.*

The seed that has reached the womb becomes a part of the mother as intimately connected with her as her various internal organs, like her heart or her liver. Since the seed has become the part and parcel of her, she is unconscious of its presence in her and it does not give her any special agony. In time it grows and all along she, with the food assimilated by her, nourishes the essence of her husband that has reached its present field of development in her womb.

सा भावयित्री भावयितव्या भवति ।
तं स्त्री गर्भं बिभर्ति ।
सोऽग्र एव कुमारं जन्मनोऽग्रेऽधिभावयति ।
स यत्कुमारं जन्मनोऽग्रे-
अधिभावयत्यात्मानमेव
तद्भावयत्येषां लोकानां सन्तत्या ।
एवं संतता हीमे लोकाः
तदस्य द्वितीयं जन्म ॥ ३ ॥

Sā bhāvayitri bhāvayitavyā bhavati,
taṁ strī garbhaṁ bibharti,
so'gra eva kumāraṁ janmano'gre-'dhibhāvayati,
sa yatkumāraṁ janmano'gre-
adhibhāvayaty-ātmānam-eva
tad-bhāvayaty-eṣāṁ lokānāṁ santatyā,
evaṁ santatā hīme lokāḥ
tadasya dvitīyaṁ janma.

सा *sā* = she; भावयित्री *bhāvayitri* = nourisher (of the foetus); भावयितव्या *bhāvayitavyā* = fit to well-nourish; भवति *bhavati* = becomes; तम् *tam* = him (her husband); स्त्री *strī* = the woman; गर्भम् *garbham* = an embryo in her womb; बिभर्ति *bibharti* = bears; सः *saḥ* = he (the father); अग्रे *agre* = before; एव *eva* = itself; कुमारम् *kumāram* = child; जन्मनः *janmanaḥ* = birth; अग्रे

agre = before; अधि *adhi* = after (birth); भावयति *bhāvayati* = nourishes; स: *saḥ* = he (the father); यत् *yat* = which; कुमारम् *kumāram* = child; जन्मन: *janmanaḥ* = birth; अग्रे *agre* = before; अधिभावयति *adhibhāvayati* = nourishes (after birth); आत्मानम् *ātmānam* = himself; एव *eva* = alone; तत् *tat* = that; भावयति *bhāvayati* = nourishes; एषाम् *eṣām* = of these; लोकानाम् *lokānām* = of worlds; सन्तत्या *santatyā* = for the continuation; एवम् *evam* = thus; संतता *saṁtatā* = continued; हि *hi* = verily; इमे *ime* = these; लोका: *lokāḥ* = worlds; तत् *tat* = that; अस्य *asya* = his (father's); द्वितीयम् *dvitīyam* = second; जन्म *janma* = birth.

3. *Since she (the mother) becomes the nourisher of his (her husband's) Self within her, she also becomes fit to be well-nourished. The woman bears him (her husband) as an embryo in her womb. He, the father, nourishes the child before and after its birth. In that he nourishes the child from its birth onwards, he but nourishes his own self, for the continuation of these worlds; thus are these worlds continued. This is his second birth.*

The mother nourishes the child not only physically, but also mentally as we have already seen, with her assimilated food and with the quality of her constant thoughts. Since the child in the womb is nothing other than its father's own essence, he has got to feel, in fact, a great debt of gratitude to his wife who is providing for himself an asylum to grow and express, in due time, as his own son. Since she nourishes the child in her womb, she is to be nourished well and lovingly nursed before, during and after her confinement.

Here we are told that this is the sacred basis upon which the sanctity of marriage is to be recognised by the *Hindū-s*. Marriage is not a contract into which male flesh has entered into the female flesh for the lusty happiness arising from a biological function, purely flesh-fleshy. The secular age of our times, fed upon the sex absurdities of the Freudian psychology, is digging their own suicidal graves for all their domestic happiness and social and national cohesion because of this shattering ignorance of the sanctity of the marriage.

To the *Hindū-s* marriage is a sacramental tie under the roof of love, tied in the presence of Truth and Divinity. Their relationship is not a contract between two parties who have entered into it, at the table of a clerk around one street corner, for a piece of legalised prostitution, which in another street, at another table, they can, by mutual consent readily annul!!

World constituted on such fallacious arguments and customs slowly walk into the levels of animals-vegetation—I call it the 'animal-vegetation' deliberately because the Vegetable kingdom has its own morality, and the Animal World has its own instinctive laws of choice at least! Such a generation of immoral men multiply inordinately inspite of all their family-planning schemes, and breed children of lust, and neglect them on the streets with irresponsibility and utter callousness.

To decry the *Vedik* period that it did not respect women is to hoot high our own ignorance of our sacred literature. No doubt the *Ṛṣī-s* did not allow women to be misused as drivers and policemen, as soldiers and pilots, as servants of the society in cutting wood and drawing water. But they were unquestioned queens of their homes, the divine mothers of their society, mistresses of their world, to whom, in a loyalty motivated by love, tempered by consideration, honeyed by sympathy and devotion, sweetened by understanding, the menfolk paid their homage.

Let us not digress upon it. Here the loving advice is that an householder should nourish the mother of his son; because she nourishes his son in her womb. It is the father's moral duty to feed the child and to nourish it not only during its pre-natal condition but also afterwards. Here the word "nourish" is used in the largest sense of the term which includes not only the physical nourishment but also the mental and the intellectual development of the child.

Therefore, the father has a great duty to cater to the bodily development of the child and also to provide him with enough chances to grow mentally and intellectually. In thus nourshing the child he is, but, nourishing himself, as the child is not anyone different from himself. None of us feels it a great responsibility that we have to tend, fatten and protect our right hand or our left leg, because any harm happened to any of the parts of our limbs in us is a harm suffered by ourselves. Similarly, educating the child, clothing and feeding him etc., are not merely a responsibility of the father, but in doing so, he is, in fact, helping but himself to express and re-live himself in the son.

The attempt of the Master is to make the father realise his oneness at least with his own son. If this feeling is born in us it will develop in our minds and the capacity to realise more intensively the *vedāntik* ideal of the oneness of the Universe. A mere lip-*vedāntism* helps none just as by repeating or chanting the item of a menu-card our hunger is not satiated.

This intimate relationship between the father and the son is a very healthy and useful training for an ordinary householder preparing him to grow to greater heights and to come to feel the oneness that underlies the pluralistic phenomena.

This sperm grown, by now into a fully developed foetus is now born into the outer world as a child and this becomes his second birth. It is to be noted carefully here that a child can be either a son or a daughter; there is no over-emphasis in the *Vedā-s* of any kind special recognition of divinity in man. The father is the seed himself; not only in his but also in his daughter; since the form of a seed was first born into the womb and from there the same grows and, in its own fullness, has emerged out now as a child. Therefore, the child is only the second stage in the metamorphosis of the father himself.

सोऽस्यायमात्मा पुण्येभ्यः
कर्मभ्यः प्रतिधीयते ।
अथास्यायमितर आत्मा
कृतकृत्यो वयोगतः प्रैति ।
स इतः प्रयन्नेव पुनर्जायते
तदस्य तृतीयं जन्म ॥ ४ ॥

So-'syāyam-ātmā puṇyebhyaḥ
karma-bhyaḥ prati-dhīyate,
athā-syāyam-itara ātmā
kṛta-kṛtyo vayogataḥ praiti,
sa itaḥ prayanneva punar-jāyate
tadasya tṛtīyaṁ janma.

सः *saḥ* = he (the son); अस्य *asya* = of his (father's own); अयम् *ayam* = this; आत्मा *ātmā* = Self; पुण्येभ्यः *puṇyebhyaḥ* = for good; कर्मभ्यः *karmabhyaḥ* = duties; प्रतिधीयते *pratidhīyate* = is initiated; अथ *atha* = then; अस्य *asya* = this (son); अयम् *ayam* = this (father); इतर *itara* = other; आत्मा *ātmā* = Self; कृतकृत्यः *kṛtakṛtyaḥ* = sense of inward satisfaction; वयोगतः *vayogataḥ* = having reached ripe old age; प्रैति *praiti* = departs; सः = he; इतः *itaḥ* = from here; प्रयन् *prayan* = having departed; एव *eva* = alone; पुनः *punaḥ* = again; जायते *jāyate* = is born; तत् *tat* = that; अस्य *asya* = his; तृतीयम् *tṛtīyam* = third; जन्म *janma* = birth.

4. *That son who is the father's own self is put in the father's place for the performance of the pious deeds. Then this other self of the boy (the father), having done its duties, and having reached a ripe old age, dies away. After the death indeed, he is born again. This is his third birth.*

When the child, who had been nourished by the father during its pre-natal, natal and post-natal existence, comes to his right age, well-educated, obedient and healthy, the boy is initiated into the duties of the home, wherein he becomes a true substitute for the father.

Traditionally a *brāhmaṇa*, has to maintain his fire and perform special ritualistic functions as a house-holder, apart from his daily divine services, at home. When the body comes of age the father retires from the field of ritualism and appoints his son as his representative in both the *Nitya* (daily) and *Naimittika* (special) rites of a house-holder.

Unfortunately, these are the days when even the *brāhmaṇa* is not generally performing these divine duties (*Nitya-naimittika-karmā-s*), but, instead, he has to go to the market-place, or to some office where he has to strain as best as he can to eke out a living for himself. Under such circumstances we need not translate the scripture to exclude the modern times; for, a religion cannot fulfil itself unless it can serve all people at all times.

Extending the application of the import of the *mantra*, we may say that the father, after educating the child retires himself from his life's activities substituting the son in his particular walk of life. Thus a doctor may retire leaving his nursing home to his son just as Mill-owner may do the same peacefully, handing over the administration or the proprietorship of his factory to his son.

But this healthy instinct of retirement does not happen is these vain-glorious days when man has forgotten how to make use of his leisure, and wants to continue in his office even on the day of his death. These days, retirement is only, perhaps, after death; however respected and revered may be a Judge, or a doctor, a professor, or an engineer, all of them are bound to continue their profession under one excuse or the other even when the society has declared him fit to retire.

In the healthier days of *Vedik* period, the generation always panted for a chance to retire from his grosser activities of earning and spending, hoarding and watching, breeding and suffering—they made use of their retirement very efficiently and profitably in their own cultural self-development, and came to enjoy the consequent mastery over themselves.

A healthy father thus having reared up his children, when he comes of age, retires, giving the rein of his office to the eldest. This old father in the ripeness of his age, smiling in a glaring sense of inward satisfaction (*kṛta-kṛtyatā*)[1] quietly departs, surrounded by his family and mourned by the society. The departed *Jīva* again seeks its identity with another suitable form in a fitting external atmosphere to eke out its required set of experiences, and this birth of the departed father again in the world "is his third birth."

By explaining thus, as *Śaṅkara* says, the *Ṛṣi's* attempt is to make the student understand the oneness between the father and the son. But I would consider it having a greater implication than merely what *Śaṅkara* attributes it to denote: an essential oneness between a father and his son. The father can be considered as representing the last generation, the son as representing the present, and third birth of the father representing the future generation, and therefore, the oneness of all the *Jīvā-s*: the past, present and future is indicated here.

Thus, the oneness of not only a father and a son, but in saying so the teacher is definitely pointing out the chord of oneness on which are strung the past, the present, and the future—and here too, it does not exclude the other layers of life represented by the animal and vegetable kingdoms. That the ground is common for the entire living world that procreates, belonging to all the three periods of time, is being indicated here by the *mantra*.

From the above descriptions a hasty student might understand that the *Vedāntik* literature as described in this

1. The exhilarating sense of peaceful satisfaction that comes to bless one when one feels that has done all that is to be done.

section, is giving an undue importance to the physical structure and its reproductory methods; also the processes of death and birth. The following *mantra* gives us a clue that though birth and death are only with reference to the body, in its essence the spirit is the theme of our scripture and that alone in the concern of the *Ṛṣī-s* while discoursing upon the *Vedāntik* literature.

तदुक्तमृषिणा—
गर्भे नु सन्नन्वेषामवेदमहं
देवानां जनिमानि विश्वा ।
शतं मा पुर आयसीररक्षन्नधः
श्येनो जवसा निरदीयमिति ।
गर्भ एवैतच्छयानो
वामदेव एवमुवाच ॥ ५ ॥

Tad-uktam-ṛṣiṇā—

garbhe nu sann-anveṣām-avedam-ahaṁ
devānāṁ janimāni viśvā,
śataṁ mā pura āyasīr-arakṣann-adhaḥ
śyeno javasā niradīya-miti,
garbha evaitac-chayāno
vāmadeva evam-uvāca.

तत् *tat* = that; उक्तम् *uktam* = said; ऋषिणा *ṛṣiṇā* = by a *Ṛṣi*.

गर्भे *garbhe* = in the womb; नु *nu* = yet; सन् *san* = being; एषाम् *eṣām* = these; अनु अवेदम् *anu avedam* = knew well; अहम् *aham* = I; देवानाम् *devānām* = of the gods; जनिमानि *janimāni* = births; विश्वा *viśvā* = all; शतम् *śatam* = hundred; मा *mā* = me; पुरः *puraḥ* = citadels; आयसीः *āyasīḥ* = made of iron; अरक्षन् *arakṣan* = confined, guarded; अधः *adhaḥ* = down, below (dawn of wisdom); श्येनः *śyenaḥ* = a hawk; जवसा *javasā* = with swiftness; निरदीयम् *niradīyam* = I flew; इति *iti* = that; गर्भ *garbha* = in the womb;

एव *eva* = even; एतत् *etat* = this; शयानः *śayānaḥ* = lying; वामदेवः *vāmadevaḥ* = *Vāmadeva*; एवम् *evam* = thus; उवाच *uvāca* = said.

5. *As to this, it has been said by a* Ṛṣi—

Being yet in embryo, I knew well, All the births of these gods! A hundred iron citadels confined me down, And yet, like a hawk with swiftness, forth I flew! Thus spoke Vāmadeva *even while lying in the womb.*

The students of the *Upaniṣad-s* never felt satisfied if any new idea was directly explained to them by a teacher. Thus, the student questioningly looked at the Master to know if the idea expressed by the *Ṛṣi* though revolutionary, had any *Vedik* sanction behind it. As soon as the teacher saw this characteristic hesitation of the students in accepting a mere intellectual theory as a philosophy until it was proved and supported by corresponding ideas in the scriptures, the *Ṛṣi* gave out this *mantra* now under discussion. This is a *Vedik* verse belonging to *Ṛg Veda*[1] which reports the declaration which *Ṛṣi Vāmadeva* made even while he was in the womb of his mother.

From the fact that in the very womb *Vāmadeva* realised the Self, as it is indicated here, it only makes us understand that the Supreme can be realised, not only in any of the different 'stages-of-life' (*Āśrama*) but even in the pre-natal existence, if one chooses to realise it.

Since *Vāmadeva* came to experience the Consciousness in him to be the Self in him, even while in the womb, and to that extent, since he could witness the growth of the various sheaths of *matter* (*Kośā-s*), and the development of the different *indriyā-s* and the slow flowering forth of the 'faculties that go into the composition of a full man," he

---

* *Ṛg Veda* No. IV-27-1.

declared, "*I knew all the births of the gods.*" We have already indicated that *Deva* means the 'illuminator.'

Even though the great *Ṛṣi* had his illumination, he complains in his open hearted way that he used to get now and then identified with the different *matter*-envelopments and thus come to feel himself confined in a "*hundred iron citadel.*" Thus the glory of *Vāmadeva* was not in never feeling identified with *matter*, but in his capacity to rise above those identifications each time he fell a victim to it. In his own words he says in the *mantra* that like a hawk, each time, he rose above the levels at which he had been confined, and held himself aloft in the serener heights of tranquillity and freedom.

स एवं विद्वानस्माच्छरीरभेदात्
ऊर्ध्व उत्क्राम्यामुष्मिन् स्वर्गे
लोके सर्वान् कामानाप्त्वामृतः
समभवत् समभवत् ॥ ६ ॥

(यथा स्थानं गर्भिण्यः)

इति द्वितीयोऽध्यायः

Sa evaṁ vidvān-asmāc-charīra-bhedāt
ūrdhva utkrāmyā-muṣmin svarge
loke sarvān kāmān-āptvā-mṛtaḥ
sama-bhavat samabhavat.

(Yathā sthānaṁ garbhiṇyaḥ)

Iti dvitīyo'dhyāyaḥ.

सः *saḥ* = He (*Vāmadeva Ṛṣi*); एवम् *evam* = thus; विद्वान् *vidvān* = having realised; अस्मात् *asmāt* = from this; शरीरभेदात् *śarīra-bhedāt* = after the destruction of the body; ऊर्ध्वः *ūrdhvaḥ*

= upward; उत्क्राम्य *utkrāmya* = having betaken, ascended; अमुष्मिन् *amuṣmin* = in this; स्वर्गे लोके *svarge loke* = heaven; सर्वान् *sarvān* = all; कामान् *kāmān* = desires; आप्त्वा *āptvā* = having attained; अमृत: *amṛtaḥ* = immortal; समभवत् *samabhavat* = became; समभवत् *samabhavat* = became (immortal).

[यथा *yathā* = as (before); स्थानम् *sthānam* = (take) place; गर्भिण्य: *garbhiṇyaḥ* = pregnant women.]

6. *He,* Ṛṣi Vāmadeva, *realising this* Ātman, *betook on his upward path and after the destruction of the body, attained all desires in the heavenly world and become immortal—became immortal.*

(Pregnant women, please take seats.)

This section concludes here when Sage *Aitareya* indicates the crowning success in *Vāmadeva's* biography. The *Ṛṣi* having realised the Self, lost all his identifications with his body, mind and intellect, and got himself awakened to the Divine Consciousness which is his Immortal Real Nature. It is a very well-known statement of the *Upaniṣad* that "*the knower of the Self becomes the Self.*" The Gold-knowing chain becomes gold: the clay-knowing pot becomes clay; the Ocean-realised waves become the Ocean; the Self-realised ego becomes the Self. To the awakened, there is no more threats of the dream-lion.

Thus having realised the Self, the individual no more can get back into his mis-conceptions and false identifications. Therefore, the *mantra* says, "after the destruction of the body." This word is construed by a section of *Vedāntin-s* themselves to mean "after the physical death of the seeker, he comes to experience Immortality." *Śaṅkara*, quite logically smashes this argument and proves to the hilt that the *experience of the Infinite is now and here*, and after that experience there is a saintly life technically termed as "*Jīvan Mukta*," the life of the liberated god-man.

This meaning is evidently clear from the particular word used in this *mantra: Śarīra-bheda* meaning 'separation from the body.' This separation is not the separation of the subtle body from the physical structure which is ordinarily called the death of the physical entity. The misunderstanding over the Reality, that it is nothing other than *matter*-envelopments is the body-consciousness, and to get released from this feeling or sorrow-ridden identification, created out of one's own delusion is indicated here by *Śarīra-bheda.*

A delusion can end only with the true knowledge; where light has come, darkness must quit. Therefore, once realisation has taken place, thereafter even if that saint carries a body along with him he is perfectly at freedom from his body idea. He may make use of his body and intellect, as an owner makes use of a vehicle for the purpose of easy transport.

Similarly a *Śaṅkara* or a *Rāmakṛṣṇa* may make use of his physical structure, mind and intellect for blessing their generation, and the generations that will follow, but such perfected Masters are no more victims to *matter*, but they revel as the Masters-of-*matter.*

In this knowledge-born-detachment the entity comes to experience in the "infinite heaven," meaning in the experience of the Absolute, an exhaustive satisfaction of all his desires. We have already seen in our introductory talks[1] that ignorance of the all-full nature breeds desires (*kāma*) which in its turn generates the thoughts, expressed in the outer world are actions (*karma*) performed by the individual. When knowledge (*Vidyā*) has reached to remove the delusion (*Avidyā*), no more can the products of the delusion such as desires (*kāma*) come to manifest.

Thus, the *mantra* explains the condition of liberation when it says that he attains "*all desires in the heavenly world.*" Here the heavenly world is naturally nothing other

1. Refer Introduction to Discourses on *Īśa* and *Kena Upaniṣad-s,*

than the All Blissful experience of the Infinite Perfection when the self interviews the Self and comes to recognise its homogeneous nature, and *becomes immortal.*

Mortality is the destiny of the finite. That which is limited is ephemeral and must necessarily die away. But the truth which is all-pervading can have no change and would, therefore, be immortal. The truth-aspect in the individual when it identifies with the finite *matter* comes to experience the mortality. When this delusory identification has ended at the dawn of wisdom, the Self as the Self must necessarily attain the State of Immortality. The realm of the Self lies beyond the reach of death.

Here at the end of the section, we have again the instruction almost reading like a stage direction which requests the retired pregnant women to re-assemble to listen to the last concluding section which Sage *Aitareya* has yet to declare. In view of our exhaustive treatment of this "stage direction" in the beginning of the section, there is very little justification for our further indulgence here.

CHAPTER III

Section i - प्रथम खण्ड

कोऽयमात्मेति वयमुपास्महे । कतरः स आत्मा ।
येन वा पश्यति येन वा श्रृणोति
येन वा गन्धानाजिघ्रति येन वा वाचं व्याकरोति
येन वा स्वादु चास्वादु च विजानाति ॥ १ ॥

Ko'yam-ātmeti vayam-upāsmahe, kataraḥ sa ātmā,
yena vā paśyati yena vā śṛṇoti
yena vā gandhānā-jighrati yena vā vācaṁ vyākaroti
yena-vā svādu cāsvādu ca vijānāti.

कः *kaḥ* = who; अयम् *ayam* = this; आत्मा *ātmā* = Self; इति *iti* = that; वयम् *vayam* = we; उपास्महे *upāsmahe* = worship; कतरः *kataraḥ* = which of the two (Self-s mentioned in the previous chapter); सः *saḥ* = that; आत्मा *ātmā* = Self; येन *yena* = by whom; वा *vā* = or; पश्यति *paśyati* = sees; येन *yena* = by whom; वा *vā* = or; श्रृणोति *śṛṇoti* = hears; येन *yena* = by whom; वा *vā* = or; गन्धान् *gandhān* = fragrance; आजिघ्रति *ājighrati* = smells; येन *yena* = by whom; वा *vā* = or; वाचम् *vācam* = speech; व्याकरोति *vyākaroti* = utters; येन *yena* = by whom; वा *vā* = or; स्वादु *svādu* = tasteful; च *ca* = and; अस्वादु *asvādu* = not tasteful; च *ca* = also; विजानाति *vijānāti* = knows.

1. *Who is this one that we worship as this Self? Which of the two is the Self? Is it that by which one sees, or that by which one hears, or that by which one smell fragrance, or that by*

which one utters the speech or that by which one knows what is tasteful and what is not tasteful.

This section provides us with a satisfactory conclusion for the entire *Upaniṣad.* The main intention of the *Upaniṣad*[1] was to explain the entire world of manifestations and through them to indicate the unmanifest Truth. All along, the *Upaniṣad* provided us with an understanding of how from the Cosmic-man the individual entities rose up as a result of the thirsts and hungers in the *Indriyā-s*. After explaining thus, the process of the body's evolution through the example of the sage *Vāmadeva,* the attention of the student was taken from the body and the *Indriyā-s* directly to the Supreme, about which it was said that "It entered within as the *Jñāna Śakti* through a cleft on the crown of the head." *Vāmadeva's* experience in the womb gave the students a practical illustration of the fact that we can end our present false notions and regain a more satisfactory and healthy understanding of ourselves.

When this much of information has been given to the students, as daring adventurers on the path of Truth, they started asking more direct questions to the teacher regarding the exact identity of the *Ātman*. In this section the teacher is trying to make them understand that the *Ātman* working through its conditioning (*Upādhi*) is called *Sopādhika* meaning 'conditioned *Ātman*." The absolute Truth is the unconditioned Self the *Nirupādhika.* The light in the bulb is *Sopādhika*-electricity and the energy called electricity is, in its nature, *Nirupādhika.*

The *Jīva* or the ego is the *Sopādhika*-Self, while the pure Self, which is experienced at the end of all our mis-understandings is the *Nirupādhika*-Self.

Now in this *mantra,* the student and the teacher enter into a discussion in which the student expresses his doubts

1. Refer Introduction to this *Upaniṣad.*

in a minimum number of words, and the teacher, a Master of his own Art, delves deeper into the mere superficial connotations of the words of the students, and tries to remove the fundamental doubts in the disciples.

"*Who is this one*" (*Ko'yam*):— The student is asking "who is or what exactly is this *Ātman* or the Self, identifying with which we can end all our mis-understandings and reach the state of immortality," a state which *Vāmadeva* seems to have attained.

"*We worship as the Self*" (*Ātmeti Vayam Upāsmahe*):— As an answer to the direct and pointed question, the teacher explains that this Self about which you are now enquiring is the Reality upon which he, in the subdued silence of the jungles, meditates upon, in complete detachment from the worlds of objects.

Upāsanā or worship is not what we generally understand by the term, because our conception of worship is only that which we have gathered from the ritualistic monstrosities which we have been witnessing all along in the various Houses of Gods. Today religion all over the world has reached such low depths of decadence that worship has lost its original meaning and has become a synonym for a kind of soul-killing, character-running, impotency-breeding, beggary at an altar! It is not in this ugly sense that the world is used here in the scripture.

By constant and faithful contemplation of the sacred Truth we, from our lower nature, raise ourselves to a perfect identification with the theme of the higher contemplation, which is called worship in the native sense of the term *Upāsanā*. Thus, when the teacher replied that it is the Self that they worship, it only means that their attempt at withdrawing themselves from the false is by constantly meditating upon the Real, the Self.[1]

---

1. Please refer to Discourses on *Praśnopaniṣad* (II-iv) and Discourses on *Kena Upaniṣad* (I-ii) by *Svāmījī*.

Which (of the two) is the Self? (Kataraḥ sa ātmā):—If the Self is that on which all Masters meditate upon and in their maturity of the meditation gain a complete capacity to withdraw themselves from all their false delusion, then, the question is asked by all the sincere seekers of the *Upaniṣad-s*: as to which of the two Self-s, one seemingly perceptible and experienceable as ego and the other imperceptible but intellectually acceptable as the *Ātman*, is the Real Self upon which meditations are to be performed for the great release from our ignorance! This is the import of the question.

The teacher in his answer indicates distinctly that the Real Self is That, which is the dynamic factor, the Conscious Principle, behind all perceptions and activities. This is as much as to say that electricity is that which is behind the filament which makes the bulb give out light, that which forces the equipment of the fan to move the blades and stir the air in the room, that which runs through the heater and makes it emit heat energy! In this example, you all know that electricity is not light, air or heat, but all these manifestations are made possible when electricity gushes through those different equipments.

Similarly the teacher tries to define the true Self through the manifestation of the Self. That factor behind our seeing, hearing, smelling, eating and tasting, that Conscious Principle—because of which we became aware of forms, sounds, smells, in words and the different tastes—is unconditioned (the *Nirupādhika*) Self. All published texts so far I have seen give the reading of *Ayam*, but some German writers like Muller and others have taken the reading as '*Yam*' meaning 'who.' In this sense the entire passage becomes a series of questions as follows:

Who is he whom we worship as the Self?

Which one is the Self?

That by which one sees...or....or....not tasteful?

In this case, the rest of the section becomes an exhaustive answer to their queries. Though this interpretation is easier to conceive of, I am afraid that in that case we will be missing the subtle beauties of the passage in which a very fine distinction is made between the conditioned and the unconditioned Self. Mr. R.E. Hume in his foot note[1] conclusively feels that the student's question, "which one is the Self?" indicates a choice between the Universal-Self (*Brahman*) and the individual Self (*Ātman*).

In fact this doubt can arise in the minds of the students of this *Upaniṣad* since there is no direct mention, so far in it, that the *Ātman* is the *Brahman*. One would feel that this interpretation is slightly unnatural, in as much as by the subtle joys of subjective self-discovery also the slow annihilation of the Ego-sense will all be lost.

यदेतद् हृदयं मनश्चैतत् ।
संज्ञानमाज्ञानं विज्ञानं प्रज्ञानं
मेधा दृष्टिर्धृतिर्मतिर्मनीषा जूतिः स्मृतिः
संकल्पः क्रतुरसुः कामो वश इति
सर्वाण्येवैतानि प्रज्ञानस्य
नामधेयानि भवन्ति ॥ २ ॥

Yadetad hṛdayṁ manaś-caitat,
saṁjñānam-ājñānaṁ vijñānaṁ prajñānaṁ
medhā dṛṣṭir-dhṛtir-matir-manīṣā jūtiḥ smṛtiḥ
saṁkalpaḥ kraturasuḥ kāmo vaśa iti
sarvāṇye-vaitāni prajñānasya
nāmadheyāni bhavanti.

यत् *yat* = which (spoken of earlier); एतत् *etat* = this; हृदयम् *hṛdaym* = heart; मनः *manaḥ* = mind; च *ca* = also; एतत् *etat* = this; संज्ञानम् *saṁjñānam* = consciousness or perception; आज्ञानम् *ājñānam* =

1. Refer note on page 300 in Hume's The Thirteen Principal *Upaniṣads.*

direction, or injunction; विज्ञानम् *vijñānam* = wisdom or understanding; प्रज्ञानम् *prajñānam* = intelligence or knowledge; मेधा *medhā* = ability to understand, retentive power; दृष्टिः *dṛṣṭiḥ* = perception, vision of insight; धृतिः *dhṛtiḥ* = fortitude, firmness; मतिः *matiḥ* = thought; मनीषा *manīṣā* = independent thinking, genius; जूतिः *jūtiḥ* = mental depression (owing to disease etc.,); स्मृतिः *smṛtiḥ* = memory; संकल्पः *saṁkalpaḥ* = imagination; क्रतुः *kratuḥ* = resolution or firmness; असुः *asuḥ* = life; कामः *kāmaḥ* = attachment; वशः *vaśaḥ* = ambition or love; इति *iti* = thus; सर्वाणि *sarvāṇi* = all; एव *eva* = indeed; एतानि *etāni* = these; प्रज्ञानस्य *prajñānasya* = of the consciousness; नामधेयानि *nāmadheyāni* = the indirect names; भवन्ति *bhavanti* = becomes.

2. *That which is known as the heart, this mind..... that is consciousness or perception, direction or injunction, wisdom or understanding, intelligence or knowledge, retentive power or capacity to remember the import of books, vision of insight, firmness, or perseverance, thought, independent thinking, mental depression, interpredity, memory, recollection or imagination, resolution or firmness, life or vitality, desire or attachment, ambition or love and such others....all these, indeed, are names of Consciousness (*Prajñānam*).*

After indicating in the previous *mantra* that the Pure Consciousness that illuminates the activities of the sense-organs is the *Ātman*, herein we are told that all the inner faculties in man are nothing other than the different manifestations of the same Consciousness when it expresses through the same mind at different moods under different stresses. On the fiddle, just as the fiddler tickles out different sounds and notes, so too, when Consciousness plays through the mind according to the stress made on the mind, it produces the expression of the different faculties such as will, thought, intelligence, insight, impulse, memory, light, desire and so on.

The list that is given in the *mantra* is in no way complete and exhaustive but in a conversational style, when the teacher wants to indicate the entire world within us, he need not exhaustively enumerate all the mental faculties but need only give a sufficiently long list to convey the indication to the student that the entire worlds of thought and intelligence have been embraced.

These various faculties in our inner world are nothing other than Consciousness in the sense that all the different types of ornaments are all nothing but gold, all the different mud-pots are nothing but mud, all the different waves, foam and ripples and bubbles, are all in their essentials nothing other than the ocean.

This enumeration of the inner world's faculties to the total exclusion of the world outside, may give the students an understanding that Consciousness is the fundamental basis of only things of the inner world. In order to remove this fallacious idea, in the following *mantra*, the *Guru* is indicating in the same narrative form the various objects that constitute the world outside.

एष ब्रह्मैष इन्द्र एष प्रजापतिरेते सर्वे देवा
इमानि च पञ्च महाभूतानि पृथिवी वायुराकाश आपो
ज्योतींषीत्येतानीमानि च क्षुद्रमिश्राणीव
बीजानीतराणि चेतराणि चाण्डजानि च
जारुजानि च स्वेदजानि चोद्भिज्जानि च
अश्वा गावः पुरुषा हस्तिनो यत्किंचेदं
प्राणि जङ्गमं च पतत्रि च
यच्च स्थावरं सर्वं तत्प्रज्ञानेत्रम् ।
प्रज्ञाने प्रतिष्ठितं प्रज्ञानेत्रो लोकः
प्रज्ञा प्रतिष्ठा प्रज्ञानं ब्रह्म ॥ ३ ॥

Eṣa brahmaiṣa indra eṣa prajāpatir-ete sarve devā imāni ca pañca mahābhūtāni pṛthivī vāyur-ākāśa āpo jyotīṁṣī tyetānī-māni ca kṣudra-miśrāṇīva bījānī-tarāṇi cetarāṇi cāṇḍajāni ca jārūjāni ca svedajāni codbhijjāni ca aśvā gāvaḥ puruṣā hastino yat-kiñcedaṁ prāṇi jaṅgamaṁ ca patatri ca yacca sthāvaraṁ sarvaṁ tat-prajñā-netram prajñāne pratiṣṭhitaṁ prajnā-netro lokaḥ prajñā pratiṣṭhā prajñānaṁ brahma.

एष: *eṣaḥ* = this is; ब्रह्मा *brahmā* = *Brahmā*; एष: *eṣaḥ* = this is; इन्द्र: *indraḥ* = *Indra*; एष: *eṣaḥ* = this is; प्रजापति: *prajāpatiḥ* = creator; एते *ete* = these; सर्वे *sarve* = all; देवा: *devāḥ* = *devā-s*; इमानि *imāni* = these; च *ca* = also; पञ्च *pañca* = five; महाभूतानि *mahābhūtāni* = great elements; पृथिवी *pṛthivī* = earth; वायु: *vāyuḥ* = air; आकाश: *ākāśaḥ* = space; आप: *āpaḥ* = water; ज्योर्तीषी *jyotīṁṣī* = fire; इति *iti* = that; एतानी *etāni* = these; इमानि *imāni* = these; च *ca* = also; क्षुद्र *kṣudra* = small; मिश्राणि *miśrāṇi* = creatures; इव *eva* = as; बीजानि *bījāni* = seeds; इतराणि *itarāṇi* = others; च *ca* = and; इतराणि *itarāṇi* = others; च *ca* = also; अण्डजानि *aṇḍajāni* = egg-born e.g., birds etc.; च *ca* = and; जारुजानि *jārujāni* = womb-born e.g., men and animals; च *ca* = and; स्वेदजानि *svedajāni* = sweat-born e.g., lice etc.; च *ca* = and; उद्भिज्जानि *udbhijjāni* = born of earth e.g., trees etc.; च *ca* = and; अश्वा: *aśvāḥ* = horses; गाव: *gāvaḥ* = cows, cattle; पुरुषा: *puruṣāḥ* = human beings; हस्तिन: *hastinaḥ* = elephants; यत्-किञ्च *yat-kiñca* = whatever; इदम् *idam* = this; प्राणि *prāṇi* = breathing things, living creatures; जङ्गमम् *jaṅgamam* = moving on feet; च *ca* = and; पतत्रि *patatri* = flying in the sky; च = also; यत् च *yat ca* = that also; स्थावरम् *sthāvaram* = motionless, immovable; सर्वम् *sarvam* = all; तत् *tat* = that; प्रज्ञा *prajñā* = consciousness; नेत्रम् *netram* = eye, that by which one is endowed with substance; प्रज्ञाने = in the consciousness; प्रतिष्ठितम् *pratiṣṭhitam* = is rooted; प्रज्ञा *prajñā* = consciousness; नेत्र: *netraḥ* = is the eye; लोक: *lokaḥ* =

world; प्रज्ञा *prajñā* = consciousness; प्रतिष्ठा *pratiṣṭhā* = basis; प्रज्ञानम् *prajñānam* = consciousness; ब्रह्म *brahma* = *Brahman.*

3. *This is* Brahman. *This is* Indra. *This is creator* Prajāpati. *This is again all the gods and these five great elements, namely, Earth, Wind Space, Water, and Fire, all the small creatures and the other seeds of creation, the egg-born, the womb-born, sweat-born, earth born, viz. trees etc., horses, cattle, men, elephants and all the breathing things that are here—the moving or flying or immovable—all these are guided by Consciousness and are supported by Consciousness. The Universe has Consciousness as its guide (eye). Consciousness is the basis of all; verily, Consciousness (*Prajñānam*) is* Brahman.

Just as we had an exhaustive list to indicate the entire psychological and intellectual world within us, so too, in this *mantra* we have got a long list which in its purview brings almost the entire world of substances within its consideration. After thus indicating the entire world of living creatures, oviparous and viviparous, that move and fly above, *Ṛṣi* wants to bring under the embrace of his conception the inert substances of the world also and so, uses the word immovable (*Sthāvaram*) too.

All these are essentially nothing other than the different modifications of the same conscious centre in ourselves. Devoid of gold, the shape and the charm of the ornaments cannot exist; just as the head or trunk or the limbs of the *ghost* cannot have existence without the *post*; just as without the ocean, neither the swallowed waves, nor the foam, nor the bubbles can ever have any existence.

So, too, the world of objects indicated by the narration, cannot have any existence without that Changeless Infinite Immortal Factor, the Consciousness.

This Consciousness which is the substratum or the mainstay, the centre within personality layers, which makes the various personalities dynamic and active—this Consciousness in me is the Cosnciousness everywhere, in every form, making it everywhere possible for those ego-centric beings to exist. We are not talking of the conditioned "Consciousness." Consciousness of things is Consciousness "conditioned" by the object, but we are talking of Consciousness *as such*, meaning, Conscious Principle that illumines the entire inner world and the world outside, and brings them within the purview of our individual subjective awareness.

That Consciousness by which I become aware of this book in my hand is the same as the Consciousness in any of my friends which illuminates for him the book in his hand. The book in my hand may be a 'Film Review' while in your hand it may be the programme of a fashion-show, while in *Rāma's* hand it may be a Race book that gives the pedigree of all the horses that are to run in the present race and yet in another's hand, it may be a sacred text book—a Koran, a Bible or *Gītā*. The Consciousness "conditioned" by the Film review must look different from that conditioned by the biography of the horses! Both of them will certainly look different from the Consciousness that plays upon the 'dynamism of Mohammad' or the 'sweet melancholy of Christ' or the 'ecstatic bliss of the *Murali*.' As the objects change, the light "conditioned by the objects" may seemingly look changed, but the light is the one and the same always in its own light nature.

In ten different bottles of different shapes and colours, the same Ganges water is poured and the Ganges water so conditioned by the different bottles may put on different shapes—long and tubula, fat and short, triangular or cylindrical, red or blue, green or white, but we all know that irrespective of the size and condition of the bottles the sample Ganges-water in all of them is one and the same. So, too, the Consciousness remaining the same, one-without-a-second, whether it is in the father or in the son, in the priest or in the ordinary Christian, whether it is in the Mullah or in the Mohamadan pilgrim—the Consciousness as such is one and the same and from man to man, this divinity seems not manifested properly into an equal intensity because of the differences in its conditioning made up mainly by the mind and the intellect.

From what we have so far said it must be evident that the Consciousness as such is pure and serene, divine and infinite, eternal and perfect, one without a second, formless and yet available for our own innermost experiences.

Declares the 'pot-maker sage' *Aitareya*, the proletarian *Rṣi*, the Master who rose from the common man. *"This Consciousness is Brahman."*

We had already indicated earlier that the All-Pervading Reality is *Brahman*, and that the Consciousness that functions in us conditioned seemingly by our equipments is called the *Ātman*. "That which comprehends everything, that which grasps objects and enjoys them; that which pervades everything is *Ātman*."[1] *Brahman* is the All-Pervading Consciousness which is the substratum for the whole of the cosmos, that which was before this cosmic man was created. In this *mantra*, it is said that *Prajñānam* or Consciousness as such, which is the life spark in human entity, is the *Brahman* in the sense that the space in a cup, is not different from and is one with the space in which the entire Universe is moving.

Such pithy declarations that provide an inexhaustible fund of changes for meditation for a seeker in the path of knowledge is called a *Mahāvākya*. We have one such *Mahāvākya* in every *Veda*.

---

1. यच्चाप्नोति यदादत्ते यच्चात्ति विषयानिह । यच्चास्य संततो भावः तस्मादात्मेति गीयते ।

   Yaccāpnoti yadādatte yaccātti viṣayāniha,
   yaccāsya saṅtato bhāvaḥ tasmād-ātmeti gīyate.

The Major Text of the *Ṛg Veda* is *Prajñānam Brahma* which is found in *Aitareya Upaniṣad*; hence the importance of this *Upaniṣad*.

The four great *Mahāvākyā-s*, found in each one of our *Vedā-s*, are as follows :—

1. *Lakṣaṇa Vākya—Prajñānam Brahma—* Consciousness is *Brahman*. [*Aitareya Up*. (III-i-3)---*Ṛg Veda*].

2. *Upadeśa Vākya—Tat Tvam Asi—*That Thou Art. [*Chāṇdogya Up*. (VI-9 & 10)---*Sāma Veda*].

3. *Anubhava Vākya—Ayam Ātmā Brahma—* This Self is *Brahman* [*Māṇḍūkya Up*. (*Mantra*-2)---*Atharva Veda*].

4. *Anusandhāna Vākya—Aham Brahma Asmi—* I am *Brahman*. [*Bṛhadāraṇyaka Up*. (I-iv-10)---*Yajur Veda*].

If one closely observes these great four formulae we can see, in and through them, the entire system of the Path of Meditation which *Vedānta* preaches. As soon as the student reaches the master's feet, he has to define what is *Brahman*, and this statement of definition of the Eternal Truth—*Lakṣaṇa Vākya*—is found in the *Ṛg Veda* where it says "*Consciousness is Brahman.*"

After this objective definition of *Brahman*, the Master turns to the disciples and directly points to their bosom and roars the truth, "That thou Art," meaning that the Consciousness which is *Brahman* is not yonder there, somewhere behind the clouds to be achieved at some time as a posthumous reward, but it *is right here and now* to be experienced as this *Ātman*. This advice of the Master to the disciples—*Upadeśa Vākya* is found in the *Sāma Veda*.

Now the student having heard the definition of *Brahman* having understood from the Master's own tongue that the essence in him is nothing other than *Brahman* Itself, he retires to the solitude to meditate upon this objective Truth constantly and single-pointedly until he discovers for himself "This Self is *Brahman.*" This *Mahāvākya* or Major Text, since it is the road to realisation for the seeker, is called the *Anubhava Vākya.* This is found in *Atharva Veda.*

Having decided for himself, from his own personal experience, gained during solitary and tranquil meditation, that this *Ātman* is the *Brahman*, the student comes back to the Master, to the looks of enquiry of the Master, the boy answers with the cheer that beams out from his limpid eyes of peace and serenity that he had intimately experienced the Truth, and afterwards he is living constantly awareful of the Truth that "*Brahman Am I.*" This Major Text, is, therefore, called *Anusandhāna Vākya.*

स एतेन प्रज्ञेनात्मनास्माल्लोकादुत्क्रम्य
अमुष्मिन्स्वर्गे लोके सर्वान् कामानाप्त्वामृतः
समभवत् समभवत् इत्योम् ॥ ४ ॥

इति तृतीयोऽध्यायः

Sa etena prajñen-ātmanā-smāllokād-utkramya
amuṣmin-svarge loke sarvān kāmān-āptvā-mṛtaḥ
samabhavat-samabhavat ityom.

Iti tṛtīyo'dhyāyaḥ

सः *saḥ* = he; एतेन *etena* = by this; प्रज्ञेन *prajñena* = consciousness; आत्मना *ātmanā* = by Self; अस्मात् *asmāt* = from this; लोकात् *lokāt* = world; उत्क्रम्य *utkramya* = having ascended; अमुष्मिन्-स्वर्गे *amuṣmin-svarge* = in that heaven; लोके *loke* =

world; सर्वान् *sarvān* = all; कामान् *kāmān* = desires; आप्त्वा *āptvā* = attaining; अमृतः *amṛtaḥ* = immortal; समभवत् *samabhavat* = became; समभवत् *samabhavat* = became (immortal); इति ॐ *iti oṁ* = thus *Oṁ*.

4. *He was exalted to the state of* Brahmanhood *on account of knowledge of* Ātman. *He ascended aloft from this world and obtained all that he desired, in that World of Supreme Bliss, he became immortal..... Yes, became Immortal! Thus* Oṁ.

Continuing the story of Sage *Vāmadeva* the teacher concludes exactly as he concluded the previous section. Please read the discourses on *Mantra* VI of the previous section.

In realising the *Ātman* within Himself *Vāmadeva* experienced the infinite Reality and thereafter, as we have said earlier, he could no more come back to the lower identifications with his body and mind. The ordinary world of experiences in which we are living is no more available for such a man of realisation, but he lives in his own Infinite experience of Bliss Absolute in himself, desiring nothing, wanting nothing, expecting nothing, beyond all finite imperfections and miseries—a master of circumstances, a ruler of his own generation—there the sage walks the earth in the strides of a God!! The repetition of the words "became Immortal" is not only for the purpose of emphasis, but it is to indicate that the text-book has ended.

"Thus *Oṁ*"—This is the traditional way in which a sacred book is concluded. *Upaniṣad* studies are always started with a prayerful *Oṁ*-chanting and concluded with an equally ardent *Oṁ*-chanting. The mere formula *Oṁ* is repeated to bring into our mind the conception of the goal as indicated in our scriptures, and to remember thus the Truth is to raise our thoughts of prayer unto it.

Peace Invocation

(*Śāntipāṭhaḥ*)

ॐ वाङ् मे मनसि प्रतिष्ठिता
मनो मे वाचि प्रतिष्ठितमाविरावीर्म एधि ।
वेदस्य म आणीस्थः श्रुतं मे मा प्रहासीः ।
अनेनाधीतेनाहोरात्रान् सन्दधामि ऋतं वदिष्यामि ।
सत्यं वदिष्यामि । तन्मामवतु । तद्वक्तारमवतु ।
अवतु मामवतु वक्तारमवतु वक्तारम् ॥

ॐ शान्तिः ! शान्तिः !! शान्तिः !!!

Oṁ vāṅ me manasi pratiṣṭhitā,
mano me vāci pratiṣṭhitam-āvirā-vīrma edhi,
vedasya ma āṇīsthaḥ śrutaṁ me mā prahāsīḥ,
anenā-dhītenā-horātrān sanda-dhāmi ṛtaṁ vadiṣyāmi,
satyaṁ vadiṣyāmi, tanmām-avatu, tad-vaktāram-avatu,
avatu mām-avatu vaktāram-avatu vaktāram.

Oṁ śāntiḥ, śāntiḥ, śāntiḥ.

Peace Invocation

Oṁ! *May my speech be rooted in my mind, may my mind be rooted in my speech;* Brahman, *reveal Thyself to me. Oh! Mind and speech, enable me to grasp the Truth that the* Vedā-s *teach. Let not what I have heard forsake me. Let me continuously live my days and nights in my studies. I think truth; I speak truth. May that (truth) protect me. May that protect the teacher; protect me; protect the teacher; protect the teacher!!*

Oṁ! Peace, Peace, Peace.

[For word-to-word meaning and explanation please refer to the Peace Invocation in the beginning of the *Upaniṣad* (Pages 19 to 26) where we have exhaustively dealt with this]

Oṁ Tat Sat

Note: **Some publications classify this concluding *Śāntipāṭhaḥ* as Chapter IV, Section-i, and count this as the sixth section of the *Ātma Ṣaṭka* as *Śrī Śaṅkara* considers this *Upaniṣad* to be...Ed.**

Alphabetical Index to Ślokā-s

* These lines are prelude to the *Mantrā-s*, but are included in the Index, the first line of the main *mantra* too finds place at the appropriate slot of the alphabetical index.

Supplementary Alphabetical Index

[Some of the verses are split in the commentary, while other important lines/statements although not forming the beginning of a verse are arranged in Alphabetical order below to facilitate easy location. The sequence of reference is the Chapter no. Section and *mantra* no.—in that order.]